Eucharist as Covenant

Pat Seaver

Eucharist as Covenant

An Aid to Christian Unity

the columba press

First published in 2013 by
the columba press
55A Spruce Avenue, Stillorgan Industrial Park,
Blackrock, Co. Dublin

Cover by Shaun Gallagher
Origination by The Columba Press
Printed by Bell & Bain Limited

ISBN 978 1 78218 098 2

Acknowledgements

The author would like to gratefully acknowledge the help and inspiration of his parents and all those scholars and holy people at whose feet he sat while on his journey of faith. He would also like to thank the staff and visiting lecturers in Mary Immaculate College, Limerick and especially Dr Rik Van Nievenhove, who supervised the thesis on which this work is based.

Table of Contents

Introduction

Reflecting on how as a young boy going to Mass in the Church of the Holy Name, in Ranelagh, in the 1940s, I would like to be able to claim that this experience created a sense of awe and wonder in me. In fact, my earliest memory was that of having to endure an unexciting, long period of time while having to stay quiet and still. Looking around was seriously frowned upon. Later, as an altar-server, I began to see that being part of the drama was much better than being 'in the audience'. But there were too many distractions to allow for any real reflection: 'Who would ring the bell?' 'Would I be the one to get hold of the paten for Holy Communion?' In general, Mass was a ritual that was an important part of my life, which gave me a status in a household that was very religious, but which did little to help me penetrate its sacred mystery. Meanwhile, living on either side of our house were neighbours who were devout Church of Ireland Christians. They were lovely neighbours, but one thing that was never discussed was religion. In retrospect, I am amazed at how little divided us.

As a young Christian Brother in the novitiate and later in the training college, the instruction on the 'Mass', as it was then, consisted mostly of short dissertations on the Mass as either sacrifice or meal. As Guzie (1974, p. 146) wrote in the mid-seventies:

> A few years back, catholic journals and newspapers and letters to the editor were putting the question this way: Is

7

the mass a meal or is it a sacrifice? ... But as the liturgical changes of the 1960s were introduced, it became painfully evident that the two theologies were inadequate for interpreting the developments that were taking place.

It was not until in 1985, when I began to study for the Diploma in Catechetics in Cork that I gained a totally new and exciting insight into the Eucharist. At that time Fr Michael G. O' Sullivan (1986), or Gearóid Ó Súilleabháin as he was better known, was in charge of the catechetical programme in UCC. It was his clear description of the Eucharist as Covenant that changed my perspective on what had become a fairly routine daily religious ritual, to a life-giving celebration that was hugely influential in my own journey to priesthood. I am now at the stage where, in spite of constantly preaching about it, few people seem to capture the significance of what I am trying to put before them. For me, the Eucharist as the Celebration of the New Covenant is so vital that I feel the need to share it with anyone who will listen. And so, the ultimate aim of this work is to enable those who celebrate Eucharist to see the significance of each act of the liturgy as part of a covenantal drama, whereby we become God's adopted children and in which we, as community, take an active part. There is also an ecumenical aspect connected with the development of Eucharist as Covenant that should not be forgotten. As Lafont (2008, p. 156) states:

> From this point of view it is absolutely necessary to recognise that ecumenical discussion invites us to accord priority to the dimension of covenant. Here covenant would be considered as inscribed within the entire Christian mystery; it is transformed within this mystery because it responds to the deepest desires of human beings.

Consequently, I think a shift in thinking and practice in this regard is very necessary. The study therefore begins by tracing the way our understanding of the Eucharist developed. This may help explain the most common thinking about the Eucharist and the almost universal absence of any connection between the Eucharist and the Covenant at a practical level. Chapter Two deals with the two traditional approaches to the Eucharist, i.e. Sacrifice and Meal. Chapter Three will give the background to the covenant celebrations in pre-Christian times, with special reference to the Hittites, whose influence was so significant with regard to the covenant relationships at the time of Abraham and which had such a major influence on Hebrew thought. By linking the celebration of Marriage with that of the Covenant in Chapter Four, the reader may come to see how the Hittite influence still lives on, thus making the link between Eucharist and Covenant easier to imagine and accept. Chapter Five, is where the Eucharist is seen to have the same basic structure as the other classical celebrations on which the covenants of Abram, Moses etc. were based. Chapter Six will attempt to examine the rubrics of the Eucharist, show their significance in the light of our knowledge of the ancient Covenant celebrations and perhaps indicate how our participation might be improved. Chapter Seven shows how, by seeing the Mass as Covenant, with its Meal and the Sacrifice, many positive changes are possible – not least a possible move toward Christian unity.

Chapter One

A View of the Eucharist from the Past

The Vatican II documents tell us: 'No Christian community
… can be built up unless it has its basis and centre in the
celebration of the most Holy Eucharist'.[1]

We, in Ireland know that. We know it from our history
of Mass rocks, and hunted priests and the stories of our
struggle to keep alive the faith of our fathers – a faith that
has at its core, a love for and devotion to the Mass.

So! What is the Mass?

Unfortunately, when you ask a Catholic – priest or
layperson – this basic, and what should be regarded as a
simple question, you will rarely get an adequate answer.
This little book, hopefully, tries to give a more satisfactory
answer.

Pre-Vatican II View of the Eucharist

In attempting a literary review of all that has been written
about the Eucharist, one is reminded of the last remark in
the Gospel of St John: '… if all were written down, the
world itself, I suppose, would not hold all the books that
would have to be written' (Jn 21:25). And so most attention
in this first chapter will be focused on the Vatican II era, and

---

[1]   W.M. Abott, *The Documents of Vatican II* (Dublin: Geoffrey Chapman, 1967),
      p. 545.

how this new vision of Eucharist has affected our celebrations. On the other hand, in trying to assess how theologians, liturgists and church authorities regarded the Eucharist, it is useful to turn to Hippolytus, the earliest commentator since the time of the apostles. In the *Apostolic Tradition* he is quite specific in recording that 'a sacrifice is offered' (Jungmann, 1980, p. 69). Such a traditional way of viewing the Eucharist continued up to the Council of Trent which ended in 1547, and was the dominant theme up to the 1960s. With such an emphasis on sacrifice, the members of the congregation, in anamnesis mode, regarded themselves as being present at Calvary. This was more than a memorial service recalling the suffering and death of our Saviour: those present in the church were transported back in time to the Hill of the Skull outside of walls of Jerusalem where they witnessed the gruesome crucifixion of Jesus of Nazareth. This had a profound affect on the attitude of people, on the liturgy, and on the quality of the celebration. The atmosphere was, in general, sombre, with Gregorian chant seen as the most appropriate form of music. Every spoken word was in Latin or Greek, with nobody but the altar-servers responding. Typically, the most pious among the congregation spent the time in 'saying the Rosary'. There was, needless to say, no levity or sense of joy. In the introductory section to The Ordinary of the Mass in *The Roman Missal*, Juergens (1936, p. 193), captures the spirit of the time and reflects the theological thinking of that period regarding the Eucharist:

> The Holy Mass is the unbloody Sacrifice of the New Law in which the Body and Blood of Jesus Christ is offered to God under the species of bread and wine. The Holy Mass is the Sacrifice of the cross, without bloodshedding ... If this was always borne in mind, with what deep respect Mass should be attended.

Prior to the meeting of the Second Vatican Council in 1963, we find little original thought. Popular theologians such as Davis (1960, p. 75) frequently made statements such as the following:

> The reason for the Eucharist lies, not in the adoration of the Real Presence, but in its function as sacrifice and food. Since Christ is present in a permanent way, the Church adores him in the consecrated elements. His abiding presence keeps him among us in the tabernacle or monstrance in a special and bodily way ...

Pennington (2000, p. 88) gives a good example of the mindset of pre-Vatican II liturgists as he describes the shock waves that were felt in clerical circles when Pope John XXIII added the name of St Joseph to the Roman Canon. 'In fact', as he added, 'seminarians were being taught that it was a mortal sin to change a single word of the Canon when saying Mass.'

The Writings of the Vatican II Periti
Many of the writers at the time of Vatican II, including one of the most distinguished, Schillebeeckx, when writing about *The Eucharist* (1968, p. 51) did not focus on the nature of the sacrament, but rather on the 'Real Presence' of Christ, with much discussion on the Aristotelian doctrine of substance and accidents, and the problems modern physics posed to it. At least he helped move us away from a physical-matter interpretation of Christ's body and blood to the spiritual reality of the Risen Lord. In a more earthy mode, Karl Rahner, as editor of *The Teaching of the Catholic Church* (1967, p. 278), writes as follows in his introduction to the section on the Eucharist:

> There is no presence of Christ in the Blessed Sacrament that is not meant first and foremost as food for the faithful people, and there is no sacramental union with

Christ in Holy Communion that is not to be thought of as a sacrificial meal.

Another of the periti (a theological advisor or consultant to a council of the Roman Catholic Church) at the Council was Hans Küng. Shortly after the announcement that a council was to be held, he published *The Council and Reunion* (1962). He makes many statements with regard to the 'Mass', but focuses more on various aspects of the liturgy, without voicing any hope for a fresh understanding of the Eucharist as Covenant. Some time after the completion of the first session of Vatican II, he writes about *'The Renewal of the Canon'* (1963) but again makes no reference to the nature of the Eucharist. Another of the experts at the Council was Yves Congar (1968, p. 175). Again, we have a very narrow view of the Eucharist in his writings: '... if faith itself changes our outlook and gives us the mind of Christ and inserts us into this mystery of unity, what light this sheds upon the Eucharist!' He also focuses on the Eucharist as food and sums up his thoughts by quoting St Augustine:

> I am the nourishment of great souls (it is truth speaking). Grow up and you shall eat me. But, unlike the food your body consumes, you will not change me into yourself; I shall change you into me (*Ibid.*).

Josef Jungmann, who was also highly influential in the writing of the Council documents, was again someone who focused on 'the breaking of bread', as well as reminding us that '... the early Christians already began to call the Mass a sacrifice' (Rahner, ed., 1993, p. 467). J. D. Crichton, another of those involved in the Council deliberations and one of the most astute commentators, while keeping his reflections solidly grounded on the text of the *Constitutions* adds little beyond emphasising some mundane facts, such as how important it was that the members of the congregation 'should communicate from hosts consecrated at the Mass they attend … (and) take part in the *entire* Mass, from which it follows that they should be present for it from beginning to end' (1966, p. 148).

The Eucharist and Vatican II

Therefore, when one reads the *Documents of Vatican II*, it should not surprise us that, when the Sacrament of the Eucharist was addressed at conciliar level, the focus was yet again on the celebration as sacrifice and as meal. The *Conciliar and Post Conciliar Documents* (Flannery 1975) contain 1062 pages. Among these, the word 'covenant' can be found on six pages – including the index. In the context of this work, the most significant reference is made, as we might expect, in *Eucharisticum Mysterium* (*Ibid.*, p. 102) where we are told that:

> the Mass, the Lord's Supper, is at the same time and inseparably:
>
> a sacrifice in which the sacrifice of the cross is perpetuated;
>
> a memorial of the death and resurrection of the Lord …;
>
> a sacred banquet in which, through the communion of the Body and Blood of the Lord, *the People of God share the benefits of the Paschal Sacrifice, renew the New Covenant which God has made with man once and for all through the Blood of Christ, and in faith and hope foreshadow and anticipate the eschatological banquet in the kingdom of the Father,* proclaiming the Lord's death 'till his coming' … In Mass therefore, the sacrifice and sacred meal belong to the same mystery – so much so that they are linked by the closest bond.

The section of the above statement that is italicised, with the appropriate citation, is repeated in *Memoriale Domini* (p. 150). In *Optatam Totius*, which is concerned with the training of priests, we are reminded of 'the spiritual ties which link the people of the New Covenant to the stock of Abraham'

(*Ibid.*, p. 740). Apart from the index, the remaining two references to 'covenant' occur on the same page (*Ibid.*, p. 759) in the section on Divine Revelation, *Dei Verbum*. The first refers to the 'covenant with Abraham', while the seconds draws attention to the way the books of the Old Testament shed light on the New Testament that was made manifest when 'Christ founded the New Covenant in his blood'.

Post-Vatican II Development in Eucharistic Theology
In the period since Vatican II, there was much thought and effort spent upon the areas highlighted during the Council. However, few if any of the periti who attended from 1963 to 1965 added much, apart from commentating on what had already been debated and decided upon at the various sessions. At this time, most commentators on the Eucharist gave their attention to the part played by the vernacular, or the use of music in the liturgy, Holy Communion under both species, Eucharistic ministers, the importance of the scriptures etc. However, little creative thought is in evidence.

None of the post-Vatican II experts did much more than develop the thinking of the Council on the structure and meaning of the Eucharist. One of the Irish liturgists, the well-regarded Coleman O' Neill (1966, p. 181), in discussing 'the unprescribed ritual which he (Christ) introduced into the ceremonial paschal meal that he was eating with his followers', suggests that 'we could pause for a moment and give ourselves the too obvious answer to the question: what is the Blessed Eucharist? It is what the priest says it is: lying on the altar is the body of Christ; in the chalice is the blood of Christ ... '. On the other hand we see some movement in the work of both Osborne (1999) and Guzie (1981), both of whom see in the *Code of Canon Law* (1984, can. 837) and the

Catechism of the Catholic Church (1994, No. 1116) official recognition that: 'Liturgy is an action ... In both of these official church statements we see that the sacraments are fundamentally actions and, even more, actions of the church' (Osborne, 1999, p. 63). A writer who has a clear understanding of covenant is Irwin (2005, p. 148–67) who is keen to point out the power of *lex orandi, lex credindi*, i.e. 'what we hear proclaimed in the liturgy shapes how we understand the biblical and liturgical notion of covenant renewal through the Eucharist' (*Ibid.*, p. 149). It is from such statements that one can see hope for the growth of an awareness that Eucharist is in essence the 'cutting' of a covenant.

One would be remiss not to examine the official Church documents on the Eucharist, especially those leading up to, and during the Year of the Eucharist. Two years before the celebration, Pope John Paul II (2003) promulgated *Ecclesia de Eucharista*. From a covenant perspective, this document is highly significant in so far as it allows all who are followers of Christ to partake in the 'supper' on certain occasions.

> While it is never legitimate to concelebrate in the absence of full communion, the same is not true with respect to the administration of the Eucharist under special circumstances, to individual persons belonging to Churches or Ecclesial Communities not in full communion with the Catholic Church (2003, p. 39).

In *One Bread One Body: a teaching document on the Eucharist in the life of the Church, and the establishment of general norms on sacramental sharing* (1998, p. 20) we read:

> The meaning of the Eucharist is rooted in the faith of the people of the Old Testament, especially in the doctrine of 'covenant' ... Our Christian faith is that Jesus Christ is the Mediator of this new covenant.

The Year of the Eucharist, a publication written by the Congregation for Divine Worship and the Discipline of the Sacraments, was written for the year itself, 2005. Seeking even the tiniest hint of a reference to covenant in this document is a difficult task. Perhaps the reference to 'Christian joy' that 'cannot be separated from the celebration of the Eucharistic mystery' (2005, p. 43) is a cause for hope. Among the recommendations in this document we find: 'A concrete task for this Year of the Eucharist, could be to study the *Institutio Generalis of the Missale Romanum* in depth in every parish community' (*General Instruction on the Roman Missal*, p. 15). Again, while this is a very practical document for all who celebrate the Eucharist, its emphasis is very much on the 'sacrificial nature of the Mass, solemnly asserted by the Council of Trent' (*Ibid.*, p. 5). Interestingly, in a ten-page preamble, while making constant reference to the 'Eucharistic Sacrifice of his Body and Blood', there is not one reference to the Eucharist as meal or supper (pp. 5–14). Pope John Paul II published an Apostolic Letter, *Mane Nobiscum Domine* (2004, p. 12) during the Year of the Eucharist which lasted from October 2004 to October 2005 in which he tells us that: 'The Eucharist is pre-eminently a *mysterium fidei*. Through the mystery of his complete hiddenness, Christ becomes a mystery of light ...' What is so obvious in all of these official documents is the complete absence of any reference to our relationship with God the Father, which is, of course, at the core of our covenant celebration.

It is a tribute to the faith and love for the Eucharist that is flourishing among the Christian community that so many books on the Eucharist have been written since the end of the Vatican Council in 1965 – many of them written by Anglicans. Joachim Jeremias for example in that very erudite work, *The Eucharistic Words of Jesus* (1976), has made an immense contribution to our knowledge of the Last Supper. However, among this myriad of books, one searches in vain for references to the covenant relationship that enables us to call God, Abba. But it is still a cause of surprise when both Martos (1981, p. 251) and Cabié (1986, p. 108) mention the fact that the Our Father – the prayer that highlights the covenant relationship – was not part of the official liturgy of the Eucharist until the end of the fourth century. And this merely illustrates how the Church, like any large and long-established organisation, is naturally very slow to adapt, or change its centuries of traditions and thought patterns. At one level of course we must be eternally grateful, for because of that cautious approach, the ritual that Jesus instituted two thousand years ago is still preserved – thus enabling us to revisit and reinterpret these signs and symbols in a way that can enrich them.

Changes to Eucharistic Celebration since Vatican II

If one were to ask what the main gains were with regard to the Eucharistic celebration since Vatican II, the answer would probably be in the area of unity and congregational participation. It appeared to be a new feature that the faithful had to learn to adopt. We were no longer individuals 'saving our souls', who were best engaged when we said our Rosary during the Mass, while the priest fulfilled his role, while speaking for the majority of the laity in incomprehensible Latin. The celebrant no longer had his back to the people, but faced us and dialogued with us in the everyday language of house and the market. The average Catholic was now part of an 'us'. We were now 'the Church' – 'the Body of Christ'. Of course, it should be noted that this precise doctrine of the 'Mystical Body' had already been highlighted by Pius XII in *Mystici Corporis Christi*, which was promulgated in 1943. De Lubac (1962, pp. 41–

2), in 1947 focused on this aspect of Eucharistic unity, reminding us that from the eleventh century onwards there is a third element at Mass that must be considered – the unity of the Church.

> Just as the body of Christ was signified more exactly by the bread and his blood by the wine, so the Church, which is also the Body of Christ, seemed signified by the consecrated bread, whilst the wine changed into the blood of Christ was naturally the symbol of love which is like the blood wherein is the life of this great Body.

Irish Theologians and the Eucharist
The Irish contribution to our knowledge and appreciation of the Eucharist is notable for the amount written on the subject. Raymond Moloney (2003, p. 117) asks the question: 'What is the Mass? ... and am taken aback by the blank faces with which my question is met.' He answers his own question with the response: 'The Mass is *the occasion when we give ourselves to God.*' We get some sense of how inadequate this is when we consider the Eucharist as God's unilateral covenant. Drumm (1998, p. 70–1) at least moves us toward the suzerainty aspect of covenant when he quotes Augustine who argued that 'salvation is purely God's free gift ... and that it is God who takes the initiative'. Colman O'Neill (1983, p. 186) brings us to a better understanding of the Lord as Priest when he affirms that 'Christ intervenes personally in the symbolic activity of the community ... to the fullest extent in the Eucharist.' But none of these writers above make us conscious of the Eucharist as Covenant. Another Irish writer whose thinking is far removed from a covenantal interpretation is Gabriel Daly (1988) who is highly critical of De la Taille's theory of 'mystical slaying'. De la Taille 'saw the consecration of the Eucharistic elements as a symbolic representation of the

'separation' of Christ's blood from his body'. Daly (*Ibid.*, p. 180), without seeing the significance of this essential part of any covenant ritual comments: 'It would be hard to find a better example of a failed imagination than this bizarre theory'. Meanwhile, in light of the controversy that has arisen over the changes to the Eucharistic Prayer in the New Missal, it is interesting that Tony Flannery (McCarthy, 2011) should capture front page coverage for his objections to some of the changes. Notable among these is rejection of the wording of the prayer of consecration, where the priest now says that the blood of Jesus 'will be shed for you and for many'. In the old translation it was 'for all'. In response, one could refer Fr Flannery to a work by a fellow Irishman, Eamonn Bredin (1994, p. 194) who points out that Mark has Jesus use the phrase 'for many' over the cup. Unfortunately, raising such controversial issues is an unwarranted and unwanted distraction. Happily for this author, there are two Irish religious writers who see that

> the Mass is a renewal of the new covenant
> in which through the blood of Christ
> we are bonded to the Father
> in a new and fuller relationship;

One theologian is Seán Swane (1987, pp. 45, 47–8) who continues the above quotation by telling us that: 'Not alone did Jesus inaugurate this new covenant, and seal it with his blood; he gave us a rite by which the covenant could be renewed to the end of time. That rite is the Mass'.

The other – a real exception on every front – is of course the late archbishop of Dublin, Dermot Ryan. He presented a paper entitled: 'The Mass in the Christian Life' (1965, p. 103–29), during the Summer School in Maynooth in 1964, in which he makes the connection between covenant and Eucharist in a very clear and uncomplicated manner. In fact, apart from a few issues with regard to his understanding of sacrifice in the context of covenant, and his ideas concerning its renewal, this presentation could be seen as merely an expansion of his thesis. His comments on the relationship formed, the holiness demanded, and the Divine help given to keep the most demanding of all covenant terms through our reception of the Eucharist, are inspirational. The tragedy is that his presentation aroused so little interest at the time, and was not followed up in either theological or liturgical circles.

Chapter Two

Eucharist as Sacrifice and Meal

Eucharist as Sacrifice

Before engaging with the main object of this study, i.e. the Eucharist as Covenant, it is only reasonable to address the two topics – sacrifice and meal – that have been highlighted in Chapter One. O'Neill (1983, p. 82) tells us that in dealing with the Eucharist as Sacrifice 'there is no clear agreement, even among Catholic theologians, as to what the word sacrifice means when it is applied to Eucharist'. McGuchian (2005, p. 1), while quoting *Concilium Tridentinum*, agrees with this:

> The Catholic Church believes and teaches that '[t]he Eucharist is above all else a sacrifice.' In the light of that, it is a strange situation for Catholic theology that we do not know clearly what a sacrifice is.

And this is all the more so, when we read that 'Christianity is a sacrificing religion' (Moloney, 2003, p. 76). We should not be surprised at this. Daly (cited in Fink, 1990, pp. 1135–6), when writing about 'sacrifice', tells us how it figures

> in most cultures and religions. But its plurality of manifestations and meanings resists general definition ... Nevertheless, of the five most common suggestions from the history of religions for the primary element of sacrifice (gift, homage, expiation, communion, life), the one most

relevant for the Judaeo–Christian tradition is the gift idea. At times however, the expiation idea obviously dominates'.

In dealing with 'sacrifice' *Encyclopaedia Britannica* (1955, p. 802) gives us some useful insights:

> Sacrifice is the ritual destruction of an object, or, more commonly, the slaughter of a victim by effusion of blood, suffocation, fire or other means (from Lat. Sacrificium; *sacer*, holy, and *facere*, to make). While the Hebrew for sacrifice makes the killing of the victim the central feature, the Latin word brings out sacralisation (see Tabu) as an essential element in many cases. ... It is in fact, a procedure whereby communication is established between the sacred and profane spheres by a victim, that is to say, by an object destroyed in the course of the ceremony.

The article goes on to describe the various forms of sacrifice under the following headings:

1. *Cathartic Sacrifice* – used to remove impurities and make fit for use, or alternatively to de-sanctify a sacred object so that it can be of common use; communal.

2. *Communal Sacrifice* – not necessarily an effort to be in communion with the god but rather to

> incorporate the sanctity which has been imparted to it ... since eating anything causes its qualities to pass into the eater. ... Where the victim is an animal specially associated with a god ... it may be granted that the god is eaten; but precisely in these cases there is no custom of giving a portion of the victim to the god (p. 803).

3. *Deifictory Sacrifice* – to provide a 'tutelary deity' of a house, town or frontier. The practice of building a city or fortress over the remains of a sacrificial victim was common in Biblical times. Sometimes the victim was alive at the time they were interred. Interestingly, after the destruction of Jericho, Joshua laid a curse on anyone who might restore the city.

> Cursed be any man who comes forth and builds this town up again! On his eldest son he shall lay its foundations, on his youngest set up its gates (Josh 6:26).

4. *Mortuary Sacrifices* – in Ghana to this present day, the chief, depending on his status, will be provided with a retinue of anything up to eight males as he goes to meet his ancestors. The body of the chief will be surrounded by these eight heads. Headhunting is not a thing of the past in West Africa!

5. Piacular Sacrifice – When a wrongdoing needs to be expiated, a human sacrifice to the god is required.

   Daly (1990, p. 1136) claims that it is difficult to escape from the predominantly negative connotations that the modern reader associates with sacrifice.

   > Nevertheless, of the five most common suggestions from the history of religions for the *primary element* of sacrifice (gift, homage, expiation, communion, life), the one most relevant for the Judaeo–Christian tradition is the gift idea.

   He sees the whole burnt offering as a form of atonement but also as a

   > creature-directed gracious action *of God*. This development is associated with the process of spiritualisation of sacrifice which in Judaism never excluded the material or external, and in Christianity, became a christologisation leading to the sacramentalisation of Christian life (*Ibid.*).

Augustine's View of Sacrifice

In the Christian context, one of the best sources for understanding sacrifice is St Augustine's *City of God* (1958, p. 194), written in the 4th century. In Book X, Chapter Five, he writes, in imitation of Joel (2:12):

'God does not want the sacrifice of a slaughtered animal, but he desires the sacrifice of a broken heart.' And he continues: 'In the words of the prophet the two things are distinguished, and it is made quite plain that God does not require, for their own sake, the sacrifices which signify the sacrifices that God does demand ... Thus the true sacrifice is offered in every act which is designed to unite us to God in a holy fellowship, every act ... which is directed to that final Good, which makes possible our true felicity ... For sacrifice is a divine matter ...'

O'Neill (1983, pp. 94–5) refers to this chapter in *The City of God*, as giving 'a synthesis of the scriptural teaching on the spiritual sacrifice of Christians, bringing out explicitly its latent reference to the Eucharist'.

The true sacrifices are acts of compassion, whether towards ourselves or towards our neighbours, when they are directed towards God; and acts of compassion are intended to free us from misery and thus to bring us to happiness – which is only attained by the good of which it has been said: 'As for me, my true good is to cling to God' (Ps 23:28).

The essential sacrifice of Christ ended with his crucifixion, but to see this as *the* sacrifice of his life is to misunderstand his entire life's work. We get a hint of his Father's mission for him in his exclamation that follows the discourse about 'the Master's return' in the Gospel according to Luke. 'There is a baptism I must still receive, and how great is my distress till it is over' (Lk 12:50). His mission was not to 'cling to his equality with God, but empty himself to assume the condition of a slave' (Phil 2:6–7). We are of late, happily more aware of the significance of the symbolism of the immersion in the Sacrament of Baptism and are more conscious of the need to die to that natural selfishness that is particularly characteristic of the human (especially) from the first moment of life. For the newborn child, this total self-centredness may be seen as a gift from God rather than an *Original Sin* – a necessary attribute of the helpless infant, whose only chance of survival is to communicate with insistence when it is dehydrated or fearful, or in need of a change of diaper in order to prevent 'nappy rash' etc. Little by little the focus on self must be lessened if the child is to grow up to be a worthwhile member of society and a fully-formed human. And while we never fully succeed in this project, the process continues until the day of one's death. Christ, the truly human one, also had to empty himself of this natural self-centredness. He succeeded, but it was only as he hung on the cross that he could say: 'It is accomplished' (Jn 19:30). Our redemption is based upon this fact – that our brother whom the Father raised from the dead is now the door through which we may enter our Father's house as his adopted children. It is this sacrificial aspect that we recall and are joined to in the Eucharistic Covenant – a sacrifice that is powerfully related to the major themes of love and unity and peace and forgiveness and service.

Eucharist as Meal
In the seminary, we were told that if a Martian should visit us as we 'attended Mass' it would have little difficulty in perceiving that we were at a meal. However, Eucharist as meal is a more complicated concept than we might expect, having as it does, a sacrificial aspect to it. Perry (1994, p. 1) explains how the humans who lived in the Ancient Near East (modern: Middle East) were told by their priests 'to offer daily sacrifices (i.e. sacred meals) to the gods who bestowed the blessings of fertility'. He goes on to describe how the Law of Moses required that a sacrificial meal, consisting of a lamb, a cereal offering, and wine, be offered to God every morning and evening (Num 28:1–8; Ex 29:38–42).

> Also, at the yearly Passover festival, the people were privileged to share a sacrificial meal with their covenant God as a sign of God's favour and blessing ... The most important of the gifts was the victim, i.e. the animal that provided meat for the sacrificial meal (*Ibid.*, p. 2).

Once the heart of the worshipper 'was right and faithful', God accepted the gift of the meal.

> The sanctifying power released by God's acceptance flowed into all portions of the offered gifts – the portion being transformed by fire on the altar-table and those kept at the side of the sanctuary (for the worshipper). The sanctified food was given to the worshipper to be cooked and eaten at a meal which was an extension of the sacred meal being offered to God. Worshipers understood that God was bestowing the favour of sacred table fellowship on them as a reassuring sign of divine blessing ... to assure them that they were numbered among God's covenant people ...' (*Ibid.*, p. 4).

The Last Supper as a Covenant Celebration

In describing the ritual that occurred in the upper room on the night before he was to suffer, no other term is ever used, apart from 'the Last Supper'. And yet, it is interesting to see the way the four evangelists make the connection between the Last Supper and the covenant. John is keen to draw attention to the fact that Jesus is the Paschal Lamb of Sacrifice, who dies at the sixth hour on the evening of the Passover – the exact time when all the lambs were killed in preparation for the evening's festive meal – the most important event in the Jewish calendar. Consequently, John's Last Supper was definitely not the Passover. The Synoptics on the other hand clearly identify the Last Supper with the Passover meal. But whichever account we choose, there is no escaping the sacrificial aspect of the occasion. The main focus is very definitely on the Paschal Lamb – a lamb that has been ritually slaughtered and that has to be eaten in a very precise way that is faithful to long established liturgical prescriptions (cf. Lev 6:9–11).

To further make the connection between Christ and the paschal lamb whose blood saves the Hebrews, John highlights the directive given by Moses: 'nor must you break any bone of it' (Ex 12:46). In the case of Jesus: 'they found he was already dead, and so instead of breaking his legs one of the soldiers pierced his side with a lance; and immediately there came out blood and water'. And yet again we have a direct reference to the method of preparing the victim by withdrawing all of the blood. 'Some of the blood must then be taken and put on the two doorposts and the lintel of the houses ...' (Ex 12:7). The blood is described as marking the houses of the Hebrews and a way of saving them from the 'destroying plague'. However, as we imagine the members of each household passing from Egyptian slavery to freedom through the bloodied doorposts that night, we might recall the lament over the broken covenant in Jeremiah (Jer 34:18). The corresponding footnote in the Jerusalem Bible, in describing the procession through the divided calf, advises us: 'On this ancient covenant ritual in which the partners passed between the two halves of a sacrificed animal, cf. Gen 15:17' (1966, Jones, ed., p. 1309). This refers of course to the dream of Abram (Gen 15:9–18) where, 'a smoking furnace and a firebrand ... went between the halves'.

And this of course raises the ecumenical issue of 'altar versus table' – a topic around which, in the not-too-distant past, Christians were very divided. The Vatican II document, *Sacrosanctum Concilium* states clearly that the Eucharist is 'a paschal meal' (Flannery, 1975, p. 177). In that regard it is interesting to read O'Loughlin's commentary in Scripture in Church (1 April to 30 June 2013) for the Feast of the Body and Blood of Christ in which he suggests 'four steps' that would hopefully 'alert the congregation to the deep renewed meaning of the Eucharist':

Step 4: Stand at the table – The Christian meal takes place at the table of the Lord which we interpret as also being 'our altar'. To bring this fact out to people, Vatican II mandated a return to the format found in all early churches where the table stands free of walls so that the servants of God, male and female, could stand around it (look at the words in the Roman Canon in Latin: *famuli famulaeque* ... circumstances). It was not 'pulled from the wall' so that the celebrant could be seen, but so that he with the others taking part could actually stand around the table of their banquet.

The Breaking of the Bread at Emmaus

Another meal that figures prominently in the post-resurrection period is described in Luke (24:13–35). As Kodell (Karris 1992, p. 979) tells us about the two disciples on the road to Emmaus: 'In this "breaking of the bread" (an early name for the Eucharist: Lk 24:35, Acts 2:42, 46) they recognise him ....' Karris (Browne, ed., 1995, p. 721) warns us:

This instance of eating should not immediately be interpreted as Eucharistic but should be linked with the thematic of eating which Luke has been developing throughout his Gospel.

However, in reflecting on the terminology used, Hicks (2009) comments:

Breaking bread is a rather rare Hebraic expression. It is not found in ancient Greek and Latin texts and it only appears three times (Isa 58:7; Jer 16:7; Lam 4:4) ... Luke distinguishes between 'eat bread' (Lk 7:33; 14:1, 15) and 'break bread'. Why does Luke use this different language? It may be stylistic, but it may also reflect some theological intentionality. That is, Luke intends to convey something with 'breaking bread' that is more Christological, more Messianic. This is apparent, it seems to me, when 'breaking bread' is only used in redemptive contexts – they are meals pregnant with soteriological meaning.

Apart from the rather dubious exceptions listed above (cf. the English translations in the Jerusalem Bible), it is only at the last supper and in the post-Resurrection period that the term 'breaking of bread' is used in the context of eating a meal. So is this term used idiosyncratically by Luke, or is there a specific meaning? Does it describe a definitive action that Jesus performed, or is it a mere literary expression? In the context of this book, one may be entitled to speculate on the possibility that Jesus physically broke the bread in a special way. This may be judged as unfounded speculation, but when one considers the Church's determination to imitate exactly every word and action of Christ at the Last Supper, is it not more likely that our ritualistic way of dividing the Host at Eucharist is a true imitation of the way Christ 'broke the bread'? When one views the way the celebrant holds up the divided host and refers to the Lamb of God, one is reminded strongly of the divided animal in all the previous covenant celebrations that marked God's relationship with his chosen people.

Chapter Three

The History of Covenant Celebrations

Tracing the Origins of Covenant

It is no exaggeration to claim that it is impossible to understand God's dealings with the Hebrew nation without having at least an elementary knowledge of 'Covenant'.

> When God entered into covenants with Abraham and Moses, He was not introducing something entirely new. … He was not instituting a new ceremony but adapting the ancient ceremony that had long before given rise to the popular expression 'to cut a covenant' (Ellis, 1976, p. 22).

Clifford (Fink, ed., 1990 p. 298), while not making a definitive claim that the source of this ancient ceremony was the Hittites, seems more than convinced that, in fact, this is so.

> An extra-biblical parallel to the Sinai covenant is, by scholarly consensus since the 1960s, suzerainty treaties like those the Hittite Old Kingdom (1450–1200 BC) made with its vassal states.

Looking at the various intersections of time, geography and literary connections, to deny that the Hittites were without influence in the Hebrew traditions would be foolish. In discussing the time frame within which the various authors of the books of Genesis were writing, Bergant's (1992, p. 36–7) contribution is helpful. She places the writing of the Yahwist account in the tenth century BCE and the Elohist in the ninth century BCE. It is from their combined accounts, i.e. J and E that the redactor chose both the section dealing with the Covenant of Abram (Gen 15) and that of the ratification of the Mosaic Covenant (Gen 24) and this agrees with Ellis in his chapter on the 'Literary Analysis of the Pentateuch' (Ellis, 1975, pp. 58–73). And when we consider the close proximity of the Hittite Empire to that of Hebrews, it should not be a cause of surprise that Hittite customs should have influenced the People of Israel. In the 14th century BCE it stretched as far south as Lebanon. In the Book of Joshua we read that 'all along the coast of the Great Sea towards Lebanon, the Hittites, the Amorites, the Canaanites … formed an alliance to fight together against Joshua and Israel' (Josh 9:1). That they had a presence in the land of Canaan is also borne out by the fact that Yahweh promised Moses: 'I shall send hornets in front of you to drive Hivite and Canaanite and Hittite from your presence' (Ex 23:28). In the sacred Hebrew literature there are thirty-nine references to Hittites. Abraham was buried in the field of Ephron the Hittite (Gen 25:9). Esau, his grandson, married Judith, the daughter of Beeri the Hittite and the daughter of Elon the Hittite (Gen 26:34–35). These instances of intermarriage were not unique. In the Book of Judges (3:5) we learn that:

> The Israelites lived among the Canaanites and Hittites and Amorites, the Perizzites, Hivites and Jebusites; they married the daughters of these peoples, gave their own daughters in marriage to their sons, and served their gods.

Neither is it insignificant that Uriah the Hittite, whose wife King David coveted, should be one of his trusted generals (2 Sam 11).

Ellis (1975, p. 25), while making no claim that the Sinaitic covenant is directly traceable back to the Hittite covenants does seem to favour this idea:

It has already been shown in a general way that the covenants made by God with men in the Old Testament were not new creations but simply adaptations of existing covenant forms on common use in the ancient world. It is now possible, as a result of recent investigations, to show that the Sinatic covenant which was made between God and a whole people or nation, may have been based upon a specific form of covenant made between a king and his vassals. This form of covenant which is known as a suzerainty pact is best illustrated by the Hittite suzerainty pacts from the fifteenth to the thirteenth centuries.

As opposed to Ellis, McKenzie (1968, p. 154) has little doubt about the connection:

G. E. Mendenhall has shown that the external form of the covenant (historical prologue, terms, oath of fidelity, imprecations) resembles the suzerainty treaty imposed upon a vassal king as illustrated by Hittite treaties (ANET 203).

Historical Evidence of the Connection
In making such a claim, much credit is due to the German archaeologist, Hugo Winkler, who in 1906 started excavating in a Turkish location that turned out to be Bogazkale, capital city of the Hittites. At this point, one must be careful to limit one's attention to the precise literary content of the cuneiform tablets he discovered and to pay no attention to the theories he developed. As Browne *et al.* (1997, p. 1120) state:

As could be expected in the early days of a new science, initial studies exaggerated the universality of the cultural milieu in the Near East. The pan-Babylonian theory of Hugo Winkler (1863–1913) for instance attributed superior or distinctive elements of Hebrew religion, even monotheism to Assyro–Babylonian influences.

During the six years of his work, he unearthed over 10,000 cuneiform tablets, many written in the hitherto unknown

Hittite language. In fact, it was only three years after his death in 1913 that Bedrich Hrozný succeeded in solving the riddle of the Hittite language. From then on it was possible to read the tablets. They were in fact, almost the entire contents of the royal Hittite archives. Among them was the Ramses–Hattusili Treaty or Treaty of Kadesh, ratified in the 13th century between Ramesses II of Egypt and king Hattusili III. What is of importance to this work is the fact that Ramesses II was pharaoh at the time of the Exodus. While this is disputed by many scholars, Alexander (1983, pp. 156–157) makes a strong case when he describes how Moses would have had little trouble meeting the Pharaoh at God's command.

> Ramesses II is known to have made himself available even to ordinary petitioners (cf. 5:15ff.). Moses, brought up in the harem, had a special claim to Pharaoh's attention.

From a covenantal perspective it is important to remember that while Pharaoh's daughter would probably be a daughter by one of his concubines, she would have taken Moses back to the harem where he would have been instructed in Egyptian hieroglyphic and 'cursive' scripts, gaining expertise in various skills and sports, learning about all aspects of his country's history, foreign policy, and especially the covenants cut by Ramesses II in the recent past. He would have been familiar with the Hittite Covenantal rituals and the treaty forms associated with them. Ellis (1975, p. 20) has little doubt but that as part of his schooling Moses would have studied the Egyptian legal system. It should not surprise us then when we read that:

> along with the Code of the Covenant (chs 21–3), a more minute code of laws, are given to the Israelites as a charter. Many of these laws are similar in form to the laws contained in the Code of Hammurabi, indicating that Moses incorporated much of the common law of his time.

Classical Covenant Terms

With such a background, is it any wonder that in the three accounts of the terms of the covenant established on Mount Sinai (Ex 20–31; Deut 1–31; Josh 24), we should find such close similarities to those of the Hittite Covenant ratified by his 'grandfather'? This is perhaps most clearly seen in the Deuteronomical account. Ellis (1975, pp. 25–6) in describing the Hittite suzerainty pacts from the fifteenth to the thirteenth centuries BC lists the exact same six components:

1. A preamble giving the name of the covenanting king along with a list of his titles and attributes.

2. An historical prologue in which are recounted the benevolent deeds performed by the king for his vassals, because of which the vassals are obligated in perpetual gratitude to obey the commands of the king. Two significant characteristics of this section are the careful description of the actual benefits conferred by the king, and the basic statement of commitment demanded of the vassal by the covenanting suzerain.

3. A list of stipulations detailing the obligations imposed upon the vassals. These include specific prohibitions (cf. the Decalogue) as well as demands that the vassals ... appear before him or present tribute once a year and to submit to him for judgement any controversies between his vassals.

4. A provision for deposit of the pact in the temple and for periodic public readings of the pact.

5. A list of gods. Just as ordinary contracts were witnessed by individuals in the community, so international contracts were witnessed by the gods.

6. Formulas of blessings and curses which will follow upon the observance or non-observance of the covenant ... In

addition to the above six elements there was also ... some kind of solemn ceremony for the ratification of the covenant.

Corresponding to the above formula, we have exactly the same structure in the Mosaic Covenant.

1. In the preamble, God identifies himself as the one who institutes the covenant: 'I Yahweh am your God' (Ex 20:2a).
2. In the historical prologue, he then describes how He has brought them 'out of Egypt, out of the house of slavery' (Ex 20:2b). And again we have a demand for their commitment. 'You shall have no gods except me' (Ex 20:3).
3. Next comes the list of obligations, i.e. the ten commandments. And 'three times a year all (the) menfolk must present themselves before the Lord Yahweh' (Ex 23:17). 'And no one must come before me empty-handed' (Ex 23:15). In cases of dispute, provision is made whereby 'you must make your way to the place Yahweh your God chooses and approach the Levitical priests and the judge then in office' (Deut 17:8).
4. The tablets of the commandments were to be deposited in the Ark of the Covenant. While the tablets are placed in the care of the Levite priests, it is the elders who are given the task of reading the law to the people at special times so that they 'may hear it and learn to fear Yahweh your God ...' (Deut 31:12).

> This custom of public reading was the vehicle of covenant renewal. There is no record of this command being fulfilled as prescribed here, though there was undoubtedly some ritual of recommitment (Bergant, 1992, p. 227).

5. Naturally enough there is no list of Gods. The law itself will be witness for them, or against them as the case may be, 'and on that day I will call heaven and earth to witness against you … ' (Deut 4:26).

6. The list of blessings and curses is found in Deut 28. As an aside, we must remember that the above material dates from the 13th to the 15th centuries BC. Bearing this in mind

> (i)t is somewhat remarkable that the word covenant is not common in the writings of the prophets of the 8th and 7th centuries. This cannot be explained by the assumption that the idea of covenant is entirely the creation of later writers; it is impossible to explain its diffusion through so much of the older material of the OT (McKenzie, 1965, p. 156).

Covenant Rituals

Unfortunately, the Hittite tablets give no indication as to how the covenantal ritual was acted out. Here we must look to the procedure that Moses laid down in Exodus (24:3–11), nor should we neglect the insight afforded us through the dream of Abram (Gen 15:1–21), and of course the vivid description given by Jeremiah (34:18). O'Sullivan (1986) obviously put these various sources together to produce the dramatic description, in which he described the Hittites and their erstwhile enemies, the Egyptians, 'cutting' their covenant.

The celebration of the Treaty of Kadesh, signed and ratified between Pharaoh Ramesses II of Egypt and King Hattusili III of the Hittites, for example, would have taken place in a spacious area. Since it had been the Hittite king who had approached the Egyptians, it would have most probably have been celebrated on Egyptian soil. According to O'Sullivan (1986) there would have been two altars at the top of an open space, each adorned in the colours and custom of the particular nation. We are invited to imagine a priest standing between the two altars, and beside him, the covenant victim – a cow or a goat. At the far end of the field, the two leaders listen as the terms of the covenant are read out, after which both sets of people pledge to observe them. After the priest has asked the animal if it were willing[2] to give its blood to seal the covenant and its flesh for the feast, it is killed, its blood collected in a basin and the animal cut in half. A half is placed on each altar, with the two bloody parts facing inward. At this point the King and the Pharaoh, each holding aloft a copy of the covenant terms, lead their people up the middle of the field toward the two altars. As they walk they invoke their gods as witnesses, calling down blessings on themselves and their people if they keep the agreement and curses should they fail. On reaching the priest, they are sprayed with the blood of the covenant victim. Both parties now share the same blood – they are now truly of the same family – blood brothers. As they walk between the two halves of the animal they are reminded of their own fate should they fail to fulfil their part of the covenant. When all of those involved have passed through, the animal is taken and prepared for the covenant supper.

While a plentiful feast will be provided, the most important part of the supper will be the small portion of the

[2] It was of particular interest to an tAthair Ó Súilleabháin that the animal would show itself to be a willing victim. He hinted that perhaps the animal might have been starved for a full day. And so the priest, with a nice piece of fresh grass up his sleeve would ask: 'Are you willing to give your flesh for the covenant feast, so that these two nations that had previously been at war will enter into a peaceful covenantal relationship?' At this point, the hungry animal stretches its neck and follows the direction of the tasty morsel, giving the impression that it is nodding its head in agreement. And a similar process is followed for the second question: 'Are you willing to give your blood so that the covenant can be sealed?'

covenant victim offered to each person. To refuse to eat this morsel would be an indication that one is not part of the covenant agreement. The rest of the celebration is one of great joy and fraternal unity.

Before the festivities end, the participants are no doubt looking forward to the renewal of the covenant, most probably in a year's time. In this manner the basic aim of the celebration was achieved. As McKenzie (1968, p. 154) reminds us: 'The covenant establishes an artificial blood kinship between the parties and is second only to the bond of blood.' The other important aspect of having a periodic covenant renewal ceremony was that it continued to remind both parties of their relationship and mutual obligations.

Parallels from Hebrew Covenants

While the above description might seem superficial, there is plenty of evidence to give credence to the basic format of such a covenant celebration. In the 'covenant ratified' (Ex 24:6, 8) we have the two parties – Yahweh, represented by the altar and the people of Israel.

> And taking the Book of the Covenant he read it to the listening people, and they said, 'We will observe all that Yahweh has decreed; we will obey.'

Then following the 'communion sacrifices ... Moses took half of the blood and put it into basins: the other half he cast on the altar ... Then Moses took the blood and cast it towards the people'. Regarding the procession between the divided animal, we have at least two sources from which this custom can be deduced. Firstly, we have the vision of Abram, when the Lord said to him: 'Get me a three-year-old heifer, a three-year-old goat, a three-year-old ram ... He brought him all these, cut them in half and put half on one side and half facing it on the other ... Now as the sun set ...

there appeared a smoking furnace and a firebrand that went between the halves' (Gen 15:9, 10, 17). As we read in the corresponding footnote in the *Jerusalem Bible* (Jones, 1966, p. 31):

> Ancient ritual of covenant (Jer 34:18): the contracting parties passed between the parts of the slain animal and called down upon themselves the fate of the victim should they violate the agreement. The flame symbolises Yahweh … he alone passes between the parts because his covenant is a unilateral pact, the initiative is his.

And this is in agreement with the description found in Jeremiah (34:18).

> And these men who have infringed my covenant, who have not observed the terms of the covenant made in my presence, I will treat these men like the calf they cut in two to pass between the parts of it. As for the nobles … and all the people of the country who have passed between the parts of the calf, I will put them into the power of their enemies.

The general reaction on reading these accounts of the covenant celebrations is one of horror and shock. This of course is exactly the reaction expected from seeing, smelling and listening to this drama played out as darkness settled on the site of this awesome ritual. This would later be talked about, retold, and never forgotten in the memory of the participants and onlookers. This would help copper-fasten the agreement and strengthen the covenantal relationship.

Chapter Four

Marriage as Covenant

The Relationship between Marriage and Covenant

While many readers might find it difficult to come to terms with the idea of covenant, many people will now be aware of the Church's shift in emphasis when it comes to the Sacrament of Marriage. In Canon 1055 of the Code of Canon Law (1983, p. 189) we read:

> The marriage covenant, by which a man and a woman establish between themselves a partnership of their whole life ... has been raised by Christ the Lord to the dignity of a sacrament.

So in Church circles, marriage is now invariably referred to as a covenant, as opposed to civil law, where it is regarded as a contract. In fact, the term 'contract' seems so inadequate in describing marriage, which is without doubt the greatest example of a strong loving human relationship between a man and a woman.

> For Christians, marriage is not merely a contract but a covenant, a spiritual relationship modelled on the covenant between God and his people – his beloved spouse (Guzie, 1981, p. 89).

And since the covenantal relationship that Yahweh established with his chosen people is often likened to that of marriage, a brief examination of the way these passionate love relationships are ritually established should not only help us see the connection between the wedding ceremony and that of the covenant celebrations outlined in Chapter Three, but should also help us gain a richer appreciation of the Eucharist as covenant. In doing, so we must be aware that while its basic structure is still resonant of covenant, there are unfortunately, many traces of the legalistic contract associated with the modern marriage ceremony, whether religious or civic.

As O'Neill tells us: 'The Church is romantic about marriage because she knows its place in the love story of God and humanity' (1966, p. 273). In the Book of Revelation we have the Church referred to as 'the Bride of Christ' (Rev 21:2, 9; 22:17). However, the most powerful use of this metaphor is found in the writings of the prophets Isaiah and Hosea. Isaiah has Yahweh addressing the people of Israel as a lover:

> ...you shall be called 'My Delight' and your land 'The Wedded' for Yahweh takes delight in you and your land will have its wedding. Like a young man marrying a virgin, so will the one who built you wed you, and as the bridegroom rejoices in his bride, so will your God rejoice in you (Isa 62:4, 5).

Hosea, speaking from his own personal married history, which is very similar to the betrayal that God experienced at the hands of Israel, has Him speaking like a jilted lover who still holds out hope for the relationship:

> That is why I am going to lure her and lead her out into the wilderness and speak to her heart … When that day comes – it is Yahweh who speaks – she will call me 'My husband … I will betroth you to myself for ever, betroth you with integrity and justice, with tenderness and love' (Hos 2:14, 16, 19).

This relationship between covenant and marriage is well illustrated by Palmer (1972) who reminds us that:

The Sinai covenant is patterned on the Hittite covenants of the fourteenth century BC ... As the history of Israel develops, a new dimension is added to covenant in the prophetic literature, and a new relationship established. The covenant is still one of fidelity, but it is expressed now in terms of marriage: a covenant of steadfast love, of love and fidelity. Yahweh is husband to Israel, His chosen bride. 'For your Maker is your husband, the Lord of Hosts is his name and the Holy One is your Redeemer ... says the Lord your Redeemer' (Isa 54:5).

Finally, in reference to the doxology that comes as a climax to the Eucharistic Prayer, Chrichton (1979, p. 95) states:

The covenant has been renewed, the bridal relationship between Christ and his church has been strengthened and the Spirit with a new infusion of life, has come to her again. So she can now through Christ her head and Bridegroom and in the Holy Spirit give all glory and honour to the Father.

Cutting a Covenant
In the description from Exodus, Chapter 34, the technical covenantal term used is *karath berit*. 'Berit' is a covenant, a pact or a bond, and appears 270 times in the Hebrew Bible. 'Karath' means to cut. Witherington (2007, p. 3) claims: 'This could refer to the cutting of its stipulations in stone, or the cutting of its sign in the flesh, but it meant that the covenant was inaugurated and valid.' And this of course reminds us of circumcision, specifically demanded by Yahweh of Abram as 'the sign of the Covenant between myself and you' (Gen 17:10). Incidentally, at the time of writing, there is a very interesting debate in progress on the internet regarding the connection between the ancient ceremonial whereby the covenant people passed between the divided flesh of the victim and the way the semen of the sons of Israel, i.e. their progeny, passed through the circumcision of each male. In one of the blogs we read:

Every individual that passed between the cut pieces is included in the covenant. And every seed that passed between the cut circumcision is included in the covenant between God and Abraham, whether they be male or female (Ask the Pastor, 2006).

However, Lopez (1999, p. 95) is more circumspect in his interpretation.

Many derive to *cut a covenant* from the root krt ('to cut') and emphasise the ceremonial sacrifice, while others maintain the definition to *cut a covenant* asserting that Old Testament stresses eating a meal over making a sacrifice.

Palmer (1972, p. 654) asserts:

Covenant treaties among the ancient Hittites were regarded as binding only when the terms of the agreement were etched on iron or silver or, possibly, gold.

However, when we read the account of the Passover celebration as prescribed by Moses, is it totally unreasonable to see aspects of a covenant celebration even at this juncture?

In the Sinai covenant we can see the basic Hittite structure. We have the terms of the covenant, i.e. the Ten Commandments. After the people had promised that they would observe the terms of the covenant the animals were sacrificed. Half the blood was thrown on the altar – representing God – and the other half sprayed on the people. They were now related by the blood of the covenant – related as family. During the meal 'they gazed on God. They ate and they drank' (Ex 24:11). The most important aspect of all covenants is the relationship formed – no more so than in the marriage covenant. In the description of the Covenant Renewed, there is a strange omission, in so far as there is no description of an animal being sawn in two, so that the people of Israel could walk between the divided halves. Perhaps this was because Yahweh was once more cutting a covenant that was unilateral. Of course one could also speculate whether this part of the ceremony had not already been fulfilled on the night of the Passover when as directed, the blood of the lamb was 'taken and put on the two doorposts and the lintel of the houses ...' (Ex 12:7). The fleeing Israelites would of course pass through this blood-spattered door.

Marriage Covenant and the Eucharist
The Sacrament of Marriage is nearly always celebrated during the Eucharist. We could put it another way: how appropriate that the Covenant of Marriage should be celebrated within the context of the celebration of the New Covenant! All the elements that constitute the Hebrew covenants, the Hittite covenants and the Eucharistic covenant are present during the wedding celebration, though possibly, one of the covenant features that is less obvious on the wedding day is the sacrificial character of the marriage. Within marriage, sacrifice takes a different form. Van Nieuwenhove (2011), in his article on *The Arnolfini Marriage by Jan van Eyck* quotes St Paul:

> Husbands should love their wives just as Christ loved the Church and sacrificed himself for her (Eph 5:25) ... Thus, this medieval painting ... makes clear that there is a lot of self-giving, self-abnegation and sacrifice involved in making a marriage work.

More obviously, we have the two parties to the covenant. Interestingly, McCarthy (2007) questions the tradition of the bride, supported by her father, walking up the isle to be 'given away' to the groom. This is so redolent of contract. The bride enters the church as her father's daughter. When they meet the groom, the father takes his daughter's hand and places it in the groom's hand. She is now his wife!

McCarthy (*Ibid.*, p. 99) sees no reason why the bride and groom, accompanied by members of both families should not 'come up the church in procession singing the opening hymn together'. This would of course resemble the Hittite procession, when the two tribes, led by their chiefs made their approach to the covenant altars. Another feature of modern weddings that clearly reflects the commercial and contractual aspect of some marriages is the handing over of the coin to the bride – something that should not be encouraged by those who see this sacrament as a covenant.

Canon 1057 of the *Code of Canon Law*, in referring to 'The marriage covenant', informs us that:

> A marriage is brought into being by the lawfully manifested consent of persons who ... by an irrevocable covenant, mutually give and accept one another for the purpose of establishing a marriage.

The actual formula used to express the terms of the marriage covenant may take various forms. Apart from 'the rigorous prescription of the Council of Trent regarding the presence of the pastor and two witnesses' and 'the expression of intention of man and woman to bind themselves as husband and wife' (*Ibid.*), there is an unfortunate lack of visual symbolism in the prescribed ritual. And of course the marriage ceremony outside of the Eucharist may even highlight this symbolic deficiency. However, at another level, such a simple ceremony can be very pleasant in so far as the entire focus is on the bride and the groom. The theology of the sacrament of marriage, as in all sacraments, indicates that Christ is present. In this case however, the couple see, and are, the Lord in each other. The ordained minister is merely the Church's witness.

Piet Schoonenberg (1965, p. 143) posed the question: 'What precisely could we expect as the sacramental sign of marriage? The answer is, "nothing in particular"'. Then he goes on to say that:

> Christian marriage can adopt any sign which in a particular culture is considered to be the expression of the intention of man and woman to bind themselves as husband and wife, provided their action in some way has a relation to their being Christians.

This is surely a weakness that obviously stems from the fact that the Christian marriage ritual was only crudely formulated in the early Middle Ages when marriage was recognised as a sacrament.

The ceremony of the rings, part of the Roman tradition, was reintroduced in Germany and is now customary and even prescribed in some official national rituals. Curiously, while Schoonenberg states: 'The exchange of blessed rings between bride and groom ... expresses very well the reciprocal nature of the marriage contract (sic) ...' (1965, p. 144), he is not prepared to see the ring as the symbol of marriage. However, as all newly-weds will affirm, the rings have become a most important symbol of the new status of the husband and wife, and certainly enhance the ritual. One could argue that the fact that this non-essential part of the sacramental celebration has achieved such significance in the overall ceremony is another indication of the symbolic poverty of the ritual as prescribed in the Roman Sacramentary.

We might look with some envy on the Eastern rite of marriage, with its procession round the holy icons, and the special form of nuptial blessing providing a richness of ritual that is both engaging and deeply meaningful. Incidentally, the procession of the couple round the icons is referred to as 'The Dance of Isaiah' and represents the start of their journey together. Of course, as they walk in a clockwise direction with their hands bound together with the priest's stole, it may be just as well that they are not fully aware of the sacrifices that may be demanded of them in the years to come, as they fulfil their covenant vows.

However, while the symbolism of the rings in the Roman Church may at first appear to have merely emotional connotations, a little reflection on 'covenantal signs' helps bring out a deeper and more significant meaning. In fact all covenants traditionally have a physical feature that reminds the parties of their obligations and their new status. Good examples are the standing stone raised by Jacob and Laban mentioned in the Book of Genesis (31:46) and the rainbow that marked the covenant God made with Noah. In the latter case we hear the voice of the Lord:

> Here is the sign of the Covenant I make between myself and you and every living creature with you for all generations: I set my bow in the clouds and it shall be a sign of the Covenant between me and the earth (Gen 9:12–13).

From an historical point of view, the sign initiated to mark the covenant made with Abraham is the most striking. In making this covenant, Yahweh is quite specific:

> My Covenant shall be marked on your bodies as a Covenant in perpetuity. The uncircumcised male, whose foreskin has not been circumcised, such a man shall be cut off from his people: he has violated my Covenant (Gen 17:13–14).

With regard to covenantal signs, there is an interesting reference to the New Covenant sign in Eucharistic Prayer for Reconciliation I, where we read:

> But before his arms were outstretched between heaven and earth, to become the lasting sign of your covenant, he desired to celebrate the Passover with his disciples.

And in the introduction to The Roman Missal (2011, LXXXV) it states clearly:

> Likewise, either on the altar or near it, there is to be a cross, with the figure of Christ crucified upon it clearly visible to the assembled people.

This compares with the corresponding directive in the 1974 edition, which focuses on the sign of the cross. 'There should be a cross, easily seen by the congregation, either on the altar or near it' (LXVIII). From this we might conclude that the crucifix is now to be regarded as the sign of the New Covenant. However, as we read the accounts of the post-resurrection appearances of Christ, it is clear from the way He draws attention to the wounds in His Body, that He wants us to see *these* as the sign of the covenant that has been 'cut' in his Body. In Lk 24:41, He shows the apostles his hands and feet. And of course in the Gospel According to Saint John, the Risen Lord has Thomas place his finger and hand into His wounds (Jn 20:27). Apart from the obvious parallel with circumcision as the sign of the Mosaic Covenant, one can also see a connection between the divided victims in the dream of Abram (Gen 15:9–10) and the Hittite ritual in the way the spear pierced the side of the Crucified Christ.

However, as an aside, it would be a pity if this new directive concerning the crucifix were to cause us to turn away from the cross as the major Christian sign – our sign of victory. Yes, it is very fitting that we should have the image of the crucified Christ in our view during our celebration of the Eucharist, in so far as it represents God's unlimited, eternal covenantal love for us. But as Neumann (1991, p. 29) tells us: '… it is the cross that is the basic symbol for the Christian, the trophy of victory …' and in this regard, he is very clear as to the correct symbol that should be used, particularly in the case of the 'veneration of the cross' on Good Friday. He continues:

It is lamentable that despite the catechesis of the past two decades, what is reverenced in many places is not the wood of the cross, but a figurine of the dead Christ affixed to the cross. It is true that later permission from Rome allows the use of a crucifix instead of a bare wooden cross. This permission does not eliminate the misfortunate corruption of symbols that occurs when one substitutes a crucifix for a cross. In doing so, we allow the paradox of the cross to disintegrate into a pitiful funeral memento of the dead Christ. This symbolic deterioration ignored the prophetic victory of Christ sounded in St John's passion and reduces the veneration to communal pity of 'poor old Jesus'.

Regarding the Covenant of Marriage, we in this society, in spite of the fact that Schoonenberg above claims that it has no particular sign, see the wedding ring as hugely important. In fact, should a married man or woman lose their ring, there can be a very emotional reaction. It is then that we can see the way the ring – the sign of their covenant – carries within it a wealth of meaning that cannot be replaced by even the most expensive replacement. For many people, the wedding ring is the first thing they will look at on being introduced. One's relationship with someone whose ring finger is adorned with a gold band will normally be coloured by the knowledge that this person is committed to an exclusive relationship with another in marriage.

In general, choosing the first two readings for the nuptial liturgy presents little difficulty. However, with regard to the Gospel, most marriage booklets leave a lot to be desired. If those involved realise that the terms of the New Covenant are identical to those of the Marriage Covenant, then they would not choose the Beatitudes, or Mt 5:13–16 or, more commonly, the story of the marriage feast of Cana for the gospel reading. Apart from the fact that the latter is a wedding which Jesus attended and at which he performed his first miracle, there is no real message for the bride and the groom. A couple who are conscious of the covenantal character of their marriage ceremony will instead choose either Jn 13:34 or Jn 15:9–12. The reading from Chapter 13 describes how Jesus announced the terms of the covenant during the farewell speech at the last supper: 'I give you a new commandment: love one another; just as I have loved you, you also must love one another.' The alternative, Jn 15:9–12, which ends with the words: 'This is my commandment: love one another as I have loved you' is perhaps less closely connected to the establishment of the New Covenant, but is excellent as a text around which to build a very appropriate homily. It is strange that neither of the two most common books used in the marriage preparation programme (Gallagher, 1986, and McCarthy, 2007), include either of these two gospel texts among the ten selections that each provide.

How the Marriage Covenant Ceremony might be Improved
As mentioned above, liturgists (cf. McCarthy, 2007) who are keen to highlight the covenantal aspect of an upcoming wedding will often try and persuade the couple to process up the isle together, followed by the close members of the respective families. Such a suggestion is usually met with strenuous opposition from the father of the bride, who has been looking forward to the special moment when he will walk up the isle with his lovely daughter and 'give her away'. This of course highlights the contractual aspect of the marriage. To make matters worse, the jeweller, from whom the wedding rings have been bought, traditionally gives the couple a special coin to be presented by the groom after the vows have been pronounced. This is the 'bridal money'. However, once the contractual nature of the coin is explained most couples realise its inappropriateness.

Again, those who are interested in strengthening the connection between the Eucharist as Covenant and the Covenant of Marriage are too often saddened at the neglect of the wedding cake. Just as the animal victims in the Hittite and Hebrew covenants, and the Lamb of God in the Eucharist, provide the centrepiece of the covenant supper, so too should the beautifully-iced and ornate cake form the centrepiece at the wedding supper. It will not of course provide the main course, but its presence should be centre-stage at the meal.

On some occasions the bride and groom dispense entirely with a wedding cake or else they settle for an unimpressive sponge or a variety of smaller cakes. This does scant justice to the covenant tradition. Even when the most elaborate cake briefly provides a 'photo shoot' at the cutting ceremony, the usual practice nowadays is for the cake to be taken to the kitchen where it is cut into small pieces and is offered to the guests sometime between one and two o'clock in the morning when they have neither the interest nor the appetite to savour it. A more appropriate ritual would involve a blessing of the cake by the priest at the beginning of the meal, followed by the traditional cutting, after which it would be offered to all of the guests as part of the meal, i.e. during the dessert. A custom that is still common is the posting of a small piece of the wedding cake in a specially designed box to absent family members who could not attend for one reason or another. There is of course a parallel tradition whereby the sick and the elderly who cannot attend the Eucharistic Covenant celebration are brought Holy Communion by the priest or Eucharistic minister. In both instances, the absent members are included in the covenant ceremony. For those who are engaged in catechesis or preaching about the Eucharist, there is possibly no better way to introduce the topic of the

Eucharist as covenant than to make the connection between it and the marriage covenant.

One of the traditions that seems to have fallen into disuse is where the groom, at the door of their new home, as part of the final act of the wedding covenant celebrations, carries the bride across the threshold. This is literally a *liminal* experience. While this lovely ritual is very meaningful for both parties it seems to focus more on the young woman than on the man: and from a societal point of view, this is understandable. Her public status, even her title, will change once she moves from one side of the door, across the 'limina', into her new home and her new way of life. It is no doubt, a very considered move. One can be in little doubt as to whether the People of Israel, as they crossed the bloodied threshold for the last time, after they had eaten the Passover Supper, were aware of the enormity of their change of lifestyle. They had been slaves to the Egyptians: now they had chosen to follow Yahweh to freedom. In considering the power of such liminal experiences one is reminded of the sacraments – especially baptism as it was initially designed and its power to mark people as totally changed, not only spiritually, but psychologically, and sometimes physically. The fact that we have become minimalist in our symbolism makes our liturgical celebrations all the poorer and this is tragically so in our celebration of the Eucharist as Covenant.

Strengthening the Covenant Relationship
Finally, the connection between marriage and covenant has always been of a practical and strategic nature. As part of the ancient covenant agreements between warring nations, there was usually a stipulation that marriages would take place between members of the leading families from both sides, thus copper-fastening the covenant relationship. The

effect of these relationships can be seen for example in Ghana, a West African nation that had previously been devastated by civil war in the post-colonial era. Now however, inter-tribal marriages have made it impossible for such aggression. The most striking instance concerns the Fantis, traditional enemies of the Ashantis, who are now so strongly connected through marriage with their erstwhile foes that they now see that any blood they might shed is too similar to their own. This, of course, is another reminder of the importance of bringing back into general use the practice of sealing the Eucharistic Covenant in the Blood of Christ by all who take part in the celebration. People who share this same blood of the Lord should similarly have no trouble in keeping the New Commandment: 'Love one another as I have loved you' (Jn 15:12). And in this regard, we Catholics have much to learn from the other Christian churches who would never consider celebrating Eucharist without offering the chalice to all present. In response to this criticism, many members of the clergy would remind us that what we receive in Holy Communion is the living Christ – full-bodied and full-blooded. Other excuses are more mundane: 'It would take all day'; 'Some of the Sacred Blood would surely fall on the floor'; 'If everybody were to drink from the chalice then we would surely have health and safety issues.' However, the fact remains that Jesus asked us to 'receive under both species' when he said: 'Take this, all of you, and drink it: this is the cup of my blood, the blood of the new and everlasting covenant.'

Chapter Five

The New Covenant

The Elements of the New Covenant

It is surprising that in spite of the number of times we come across Jeremiah's vision of the New Covenant, liturgists or theologians rarely engage in a practical way with its content.

> See the days are coming – it is Yahweh who speaks – when I will make a new covenant with the House of Israel ... but not a covenant like the one I made with their ancestors on the day I took them by the hand to bring them out of the land of Egypt ... Deep within them I will plant my Law, writing it on their hearts. Then I will be their God and they shall be my people (Jer 31:31–33).

At this point it is important to examine the way in which Jesus, as he entered the final phase of his sacrificial life in obedience to his Father, ritualised this New Covenant event and in fact his whole life and mission, in a liturgy that Moriarty (1999, pp. 35–9) refers to as the *Triduum Sacrum* – Holy Thursday, Good Friday and Easter Sunday. Depending on how we read the accounts of his passion, death and resurrection, we can see how the covenantal elements are all present in this time capsule, though perforce, not in the same order as one sees in either the Mosaic or the Hittite ceremonies.

At the Last Supper, the covenant meal, Jesus explains the terms of the covenant. This is most clearly seen in the

Gospel of St John, where five chapters are given over to his explanation of the ways in which human love and the Spirit of Love must permeate our lives and the life of the world. 'This is my commandment: love one another, as I have loved you' (Jn 15:12). It is not written on stone, or carved on some precious metal, but as mentioned above, cut into the Body of the Lord in the shape of the five wounds. It must also be engraved in our minds and hearts. In this regard, the author of Hebrews quotes directly from Jeremiah (Jer 31:33–34, 8:12):

> This is the covenant I will make with them
> when those days arrive.

And the Lord then goes on to say:

> I will put my laws into their hearts
> And write them on their minds.
> I will never call their sins to mind,
> Or their offences. (Heb 10:16–17)

On the occasion of the ratification of the Mosaic Covenant in Ex 24:7, we hear the people of Israel say: 'We will observe all that Yahweh has decreed.' Unfortunately, at the last supper, there is no evidence of any profession of faithfulness, with the exception of Peter's rather bombastic and hollow manifestation of loyalty: 'Though all lose faith in you, I will never lose faith' (Mt 26:33). And in fact, not one of the apostles was present when 'Jesus, as Saviour, was completed, brought to fulfilment in his death' (Casey, 1980, p. 11).

Jesus as Priest and Victim
The following day, Christ the victim is sacrificed on Calvary. This had of course been already anticipated at the Last Supper meal the previous night by the ritual separation of his sacramental body and blood. Here, it is worth noting that even the description of the events after his death (Jn

19:32–37) mimics the traditional method of preparing a calf or sheep, where all the blood is drained from the body. The fact that his knees were not broken reminds us that Christ is the Paschal Lamb, about which Moses prescribed: 'nor must you break any bone of it' (Ex 12:46).

Jesus clearly saw himself as the priest and victim of the New Covenant and this is unmistakable in the words he used when he said: 'Drink all of you from this, he said for this is my blood, the blood of the covenant, which is to be poured out for many for the forgiveness of sins' (Mt 26:27–29).

> This signifies the making of a new covenant. In the old covenant the union of God and the people was symbolised by the sprinkling of the blood of an animal (Ex 24:5–8); now the union is perfect in the blood of one who is God and man. Jesus' followers are told to do what he has done in his remembrance. This refers both to the ritual action and to the self-gift it sacramentalises (Karris, 1992, p. 975).

The new relationship thus formed – the central aspect of every covenant – is then explained to the apostles:

> … and now I confer a kingdom on you, just as my father has conferred one on me: you will eat and drink at my table in my kingdom … (Lk 22:30).

In the gospel according to Matthew, the 'kingdom' is that of his Father (Mt 26:29), while Mark uses 'the kingdom of God' (Mk 14:25).

It is doubtful if the apostles appreciated the fact that they were present at the most momentous occasion in history. The evangelist Luke has them, almost immediately after the cutting of the covenant, arguing among themselves. 'A dispute arose also between them about which should be reckoned the greatest …' (Lk 20:24). However, as one reads the Letter to the Hebrews, it is obvious that sixty or so years after the event, there is an awareness that in essence, a new covenant had been cut and that Christ is the New High-priest,

> whose power to save is utterly certain, since he is living for ever to intercede for all who come to God through him ... and to the same degree it is a better covenant of which he is the mediator, founded on better promises (Heb 7:25, 8:6).

Following on his death, came the Resurrection and the Ascension of Christ into heaven. As Casey (1980, p. 48) tells us:

> Jesus as priest performs the actions of the old covenant cultic priesthood: he offers sacrifice for sins (Heb 7:27); he is mediator between God and the people (Heb 8:6); he enters into the holy place to attain purification (Heb 9:12). In each of these acts he is superior to the Levitical priests: his sacrifice is his very self; his mediation is totally efficacious; he enters into the true holy place – the very presence of God; it is his own blood which purifies.

With regard to the use of the term 'priest' in modern religious parlance, it should be noted that it was not until the middle of the third century that it was used as an alternative to 'presbyter' i.e. one of the leaders in the local church – the one who presides at the Eucharist and at other gatherings. Cyprian, the bishop and martyr of Carthage, saw the Eucharist primarily as 'a propitiatory sacrifice which only a consecrated priest can perform', and so the idea grew that 'presbyters and bishops are the successors of the Old Testament priesthood ...' (1955, Yust, ed., *Encyclopaedia Britannica*, Vol. 18, p. 482). Up until quite recently, it was clear that if people were referred to as 'priests', they were talking about Catholic clergy. However, in recent years, men and women in ministry in many of the other Christian churches are called 'priests'. While this is yet another indication of the way the followers of Christ are drawing closer together, it is a failure to recognise that the Lord Jesus is the one and only priest who 'offers himself only once to take the faults of many on himself ...' (Heb

9:28). And so, as an aside, it would probably be better for those who seek justice for women in the Church to ask, not that women should be ordained priests, but that they might be chosen and appointed as presbyters. The historical reason why this has not occurred was that, up to quite recently, women were not entitled to give witness or act on juries.[3] And giving witness to the Risen Christ was at the core of the ministry of every presbyter.

Eucharist as Covenant

Ryan (1965, p. 117) makes an interesting point with reference to Christ's use of the term 'Covenant':

> The Sermon on the Mount displays quite clearly the role of Christ as mediator of a new law which would govern the relationship between God and his people, but even there, no specific mention is made of 'covenant'. The word appears for the first time on the lips of Christ when he gives to the apostles the rite by which the covenant in his blood could be renewed to the end of time.

And so in the light of the above, it may not be so difficult to see how our modern understanding of 'Covenant' has not been highlighted, and in fact, is mentioned only once in the one hundred and nine pages of the introductory chapters of the new *Roman Missal – English Translation According to the Third Typical Edition* (2011, p. LXX). It occurs in a reference to 'Communion under Both Kinds', when we are told that:

> Holy Communion has a fuller form as a sign when it takes place under both kinds. For in this form the sign of the Eucharistic banquet is more clearly evident and clearer expression is given to the divine will by which the new and

---

3   The Jury's Act of 1976 did away with the exemption that women had from jury service. Up until then only two women had ever served on a jury in the Republic of Ireland. It was only in 1975, that the supreme court in Louisiana reversed its 1961 decision denying women that same right.

eternal Covenant is ratified in the Blood of the Lord, as also the connection between the Eucharistic banquet and the eschatological banquet in the kingdom of the Father.

And even, here the emphasis is on *banquet*, which, in this single sentence appears three times. The one place where we are sure to hear the word 'covenant' is at the most solemn part of each of the ten Eucharist Prayers, when, as the celebrant bends low over the chalice, he says:

> Take this, all of you and drink from it, for this is the chalice of my blood, the blood of the new and eternal covenant, which will be poured out for you and for many for the forgiveness of sins.

Eucharistic Prayer IV has two additional references that appear between the Preface and the Consecration. The first: 'Time and again you offered them covenants and through the prophets taught them to look forward to salvation' (*Ibid.*, p. 524). Then, as part of the Epiclesis, the priest makes reference to 'the celebration of this great mystery, which he himself left us as an eternal covenant' (*Ibid.*, p. 525). The relatively new Eucharistic Prayer for Reconciliation I is the first of the new prefaces that contains a mention of 'covenant'. It states that

> though time and again we have broken your covenant, you have bound the human family to yourself through Jesus your Son, our Redeemer, with a new bond of love so tight that it can never be undone (*Ibid.*, p. 643).

Then just before the consecration, we have a very insightful statement:

> Before his arms were outstretched between heaven and earth, to become the lasting sign of your covenant, he desired to celebrate the Passover with his disciples (*Ibid.*, p. 644).

This of course reflects the sentiments expressed by Jesus in his conversation with Nicodemus.

Yes, God loved the world so much that he gave is only Son,
so that everyone who believes in him may not be lost but
may have eternal life (Jn 3:16).

'Covenant' is of course mentioned for the third time in the
prayer of consecration. 'The Church on the Path of Unity',
the first of the Eucharistic Prayers for Use in Masses for
Various Needs is also more covenant-friendly, with a
reference to 'the covenant of your love' in the preface, as
well as the normal wording for the consecration of the wine.
Incidentally, it is worth noting, the words used at the
consecration of the bread come straight from a covenant
context. When the celebrant says: 'Take this, all of you, and
eat of it, for this is my Body, which will be *given up* for you',
he is using a translation of the Hebrew word 'didomenon',
traditionally used in connection with the offering up of an
animal for sacrifice.

In describing the *Basic Structure of the Mass*, Emminghaus
(1988, pp. 6–18), indicates the ways in which Jesus set out
to follow the pattern laid down by Moses in his covenant
celebration – even to the connection between the twelve
tribes and the twelve apostles. The main point he
emphasises is

> that covenant blood had expiatory power ... For those who
> lived in a world shaped by the Old Testament promises,
> the establishment of a new covenant was part of the
> expectations concerning salvation that Christ fulfilled
> (*Ibid.*, p. 7).

He is very clear that Jesus is the 'new Moses, the mediator
of the new covenant that brings the new Israel into being
(*Ibid.*, p. 11). At the Passover celebration the People of Israel
were to give

> conscious presence to the great deeds God had done for his
> people ... they included the rescue of the people with the
> help of the Sea of Reeds, the sealing of the covenant on

Sinai in the blood of the peace offering and in the covenant meal (Ex 24:4–11) and the conquest of Canaan, the promised land. These various events were all involved in the making of the covenant and in the existence of Israel as God's covenanted people (*Ibid.*, p. 13).

This 'conscious presence to the great deeds God has done' is of course reminiscent of the second of the 'six elements' that, as Ellis (1975, p. 25) informed us above (p. 35), gave us the structure and the content of the Hittite suzerainty pacts.

The New Eucharistic Prayers from a Covenantal Viewpoint
As we look at either the new *Order of the Mass* or the old missal, we recognise this structure and note that 'the preamble giving the name of the covenanting king along with a list of his titles and attributes' is identical to the structure and content of the Prefaces and the Eucharistic Prayers in the Mass.

With this in mind, it may be in our best interest to start with the words of the various Eucharistic Prayers and then to continue our analysis of the Eucharist as covenant in something akin to a forensic method. Besides the special prefaces for Eucharistic Prayers 2 and 4, there are fifty various prefaces from which to choose in the new Roman Missal (2011). Likewise, apart from the traditional four Eucharistic Prayers, there are six relatively new forms: Eucharistic Prayer for Reconciliation I and II, and For Various Needs I, II, III and IV. Scanning through these, one can see that the same structure in the preamble to both the Hittite and the Mosaic Covenant is also present in the Eucharistic Covenant. As an aside, most liturgists would dispute the correctness of separating the Preface from the Eucharistic Prayer.

The titles and attributes of the first element are clear: 'Lord, holy Father, almighty and eternal God'; 'Holy, Holy,

Holy Lord God of hosts. Heaven and earth are full of your glory'; 'fount of all holiness' (as found in the 'Sanctus'). Other titles and attributes are found in the various Eucharistic Prayers, e.g. 'eternal God, living and true'; 'Divine Majesty' (I); 'Father most holy ...' (II); 'fount of all holiness' (III); '... the one God living and true, existing before all ages and abiding for all eternity, dwelling in unapproachable light ... who alone are good, the source of life, have made all that is ...' (IV).

The second element, where 'the benevolent deeds performed by the king in favour of his vassals ...' (*Ibid.*, p. 27) are easily found '... you continue to make all these good things, O Lord: you sanctify them, fill them with life, bless them, and bestow them upon us' (I); '... Father most holy ... you have made all things ...' (II); '... you give life to all things and make them holy'; '... you willed to reconcile us to yourself ...'; 'you bestow on the world all that is good' (III); 'And you so loved the world, Father most holy, that in the fullness of time you sent your Only Begotten Son to be our Saviour' (IV). In the Preface for Sundays of the Year I we see that God has made of us, 'a chosen race, a royal priesthood, a holy nation, a people for your own possession' and has 'called us out of darkness into your own wonderful light'.

Strangely enough when we search for the list of stipulations in the body of the Eucharistic Prayer we draw a blank. There is in fact only one basic term that we must fulfil, but, to find it we have to go back to the description of the very first celebration of the New Covenant during which Jesus himself said: 'This is my commandment: love one another as I have loved you' (Jn 15:12).

The fourth element concerns the need to keep the covenant fresh in the memory of people. The words of consecration in all ten Eucharistic Prayers contain the words; 'Do this in memory of me.' Apart from that we have various other references to our need and our desire to recall all that the Lord has done for us. In Eucharistic Prayer I, we find: 'Therefore, O Lord, as we celebrate the memorial of the blessed Passion, the Resurrection from the dead, and the glorious Ascension into heaven of Christ ...'. This reference to 'memorial' appears in all ten Eucharistic Prayers in a variety of formats that are essentially similar.

Instead of 'a list of gods', all the Eucharistic Prayers contain a reference to the 'Saints on whose constant intercession in your presence we rely for unfailing help'. It is interesting that in the new version (2011), 'in your presence' is added. In this role we could imagine them, not just as intercessors, but as fellow witnesses to the faith of the Church.

The Formulas of Blessings and Curses

Finally, the traditional Hittite Covenant contained 'formulas of blessings and curses'. It should not escape the attention of God's holy people that when they stand for the 'Our Father', they ask for their trespasses to be forgiven in the same way that they forgive their enemies, i.e. those who trespass against them! This is obviously a blessing for those who have love and forgiveness in their hearts, but a curse for those who do not keep the basic commandment of the New Covenant and are without love. We recall of course what Jesus had to say with regard to this matter:

> So then, if you are bringing your offering to the altar and there remember that your brother has something against you, leave your offering there before the altar, go and be reconciled with your brother first, and then come back and present your offering (Mt 5:23).

Incidentally, while the General Instruction of the Roman Missal (2005, p. 26) now bids us to stand for all of the Mass with the exception of the readings and the consecration, where we kneel, the old version had us stand only at the Alleluia, the gospel, the Prayer of the Faithful and the Our Father. In a way, this emphasised the importance of these parts of the Mass, especially the Lord's Prayer. With regard to the New Covenant, it is of course a vital declaration of the new relationship that had been formed by Christ between us and God – the core of the covenant.

Chapter Six

Similarities between the Eucharist and Ancient Covenants

Assembling

One of the most important points to remember when we take part in the celebration of our covenant with God our Heavenly Father is that we are a united people. In fact, from a covenantal point of view, we are unique, in so far as we are the Body of Christ: Priest and Victim and People are one. We are not a disparate group of varied humans representing the weaker party to the covenant, but a united family – a single entity in this process. We respond with one voice – that of our brother, Christ – to the call to form a childlike relationship with Abba.

But before we speak, we gather as Christ. In this regard, the new liturgy is very clear. In one of the Eucharistic Prayers we read:

> Blessed indeed is your Son, present in our midst when we are gathered by his love, when, as once for the disciples, so now for us, he opens the Scriptures and breaks the bread.

And the gathering is part of the celebration – not a noisy interruption for those pious souls who have come early and are earnestly engaged in their private devotions!

When we meet to celebrate our relationship with God, we meet, not in His house, which is in Heaven, but in 'Teach an Phobail', which translates from the Irish as 'The house of the community'. In some church porches, one reads notices that warn us to be quiet, silent and restrained. But as the act of assembly is part of the ritual, it does not make sense to join one's neighbour in a seat and not greet and enquire about their health and the affairs of the family. The Lord prays that we may be one, and in the *Eucharistic Prayer for Use in Masses for Various Needs III* we too pray:

> Keep us attentive to the needs of all that, sharing their grief and pain, their joy and hope, we may faithfully bring them the good news of salvation and go forward with them along the way of your Kingdom.

Could one not argue that a quiet conversation before the Eucharist with our neighbour is of obligation. After all, many of those who attend Mass nowadays do so for a variety of reasons. It may be a funeral or anniversary Mass, a wedding, a confirmation, or some family celebration. And yet the first task of the presider is to unify this rather diverse gathering, consisting of some who rarely come to church and who consequently feel disconnected from the liturgy or who are quite antagonistic or resentful at having to be at Mass. They can often be isolated, not only spiritually, but also in a real human way, with eyes averted and arms folded across their chests. The challenge can be great. As Crichton (1993, p. 82) tells us:

> At a psychological level, too, there is a case for saying that if a crowd of people are to become a community they need to be made aware of their relationship to each other; they have to move from being a crowd to becoming a community.

If the priest is to genuinely be *in persona Christi* for those assembled, his own approach will be friendly and welcoming.

But we must also be conscious of the fact that we are moving into sacred time and sacred space, where, in our celebration, we join the angels and saints as our covenant is made present. In the other covenants, we speak about 'renewal' and other time-based words. But when we gather to celebrate our Eucharist, it is in God's eternal now. So, we too move into the eternal now so that literally, ours is the 'same sacrifice as that of the cross'.

The Priest
Nowadays, there is a growing awareness of the fact that we have only one priest, i.e. Christ, who makes the connection between us humans and God, our Creator. And yet the celebrant at Mass is somehow incorporated into this priestly role in a very unique way. During this celebration, he is most often the hands and voice and the eyes of Christ. In his discussion of *catabasis*, God's descent to man, Kunzler (2001, p. 24) discusses the 'space between' as the prerequisite for any communication with God.

> This space between is in the first place man's bodily nature, through which he must express himself if he wishes to enter into relationship with another.

And this applies especially to the celebrant and the other ministers in the celebration of the Eucharist. His very walk, as the priest makes his way to the altar will recall the congregation to a space within themselves – their inner core, the sanctuary within which God takes up his abode. When he reaches the altar, he bows as he extends his arms in a public act of love and places his hands flat on it, as he kisses it. The altar is Christ. As Deiss (1992, p. 17) tells us:

> The priest is going to direct the celebration, but first before the entire community he manifests his love and his adoration toward Christ the Lord who seduced his heart.

The other side of the equation is *anabasis* – man's ascent to God. All involved in the celebration would do well to recall what Kunzler (2001, p. 134) has to say on this subject:

> The material objects used in the liturgy are not externals but expression; in them the hidden divine reality expresses itself and so makes it possible for the human person to interiorise this reality by means of his senses.

The priest himself, through the instrument that is his body, by the graciousness of his words and actions and personality, is the primary object that can facilitate, or militate against, the peoples' absorption into the sacred mysteries that are taking place. His whole demeanour, whether he is kissing the Book of the Gospels or lifting the Host, all will speak in the language of sign and symbol, that this is a holy place and that what we are about is the worship of the Almighty. But while the priest leads the way, it behoves everybody, Eucharistic Ministers, Ministers of the Word, altar servers, stewards, collectors etc., to play their part in creating the atmosphere that is appropriate for each part of the liturgy. For example, a reader who is ill-prepared and stumbles and stammers and mispronounces the readings does little to reflect God's word. A parishioner, who sends texts during the Eucharistic Prayer, is not only a distraction, but is a symbol of irreverence and shows a complete lack of awareness of what is involved in this act of worship of God Almighty. We do well to remind ourselves that the liturgy is a communal exercise of faith and love.

Liturgy of the Word

When we search the ritual for those symbolic actions that have a covenantal aspect, we must be careful to recall the number of times the 'Mass' has been reformed. The point can be argued as to whether this brings us nearer to the actual event that took place 'on the night he was betrayed', or closer to its development based on a growing awareness of its significance as the establishment of a New Covenant sealed in the Blood of the Lamb. In either case, if we take an unprejudiced view of the actions at the Eucharistic celebration we must be impressed by their similarity to those of the Mosaic and Hittite covenants.

Firstly, as we watch the entrance procession at Sunday Mass, with the deacon holding aloft the Book of the Gospels, we may be reminded of the two chiefs holding aloft the terms of the covenant in the Hittite celebration or the renewal of the covenant in 2 Kings, Chapter 23. And for us, this is the legal document by which we swear, containing the good news of the New Covenant.

Reaching the altar, representing the Lord, the priest stretches out his arms to embrace and kiss it. It is of interest that the introduction to the 2011 version of the Roman Missal tells us that a fixed stone altar 'more clearly and permanently signifies Christ Jesus, the Living Stone'. While this may seem a matter of little importance to the average parishioner, the celebrant who is immersed in the ways of the covenant, may find that this is straying a little from the tradition, where it is Christ who is sacrificed on the altar. One way or another, the altar is very sacred and its incensing at 'high Mass' once more highlights this fact. Then, as part of the introductory rites everybody makes a public act of confession, since nobody can keep this single term of the New Covenant – to love as Jesus has loved us – perfectly.

The liturgy of the word that follows is essentially an explanation of the various aspects of the New Covenant – the command to love one another as Jesus has loved us, the real kinship established between us and God our Father, the relationship between all people, our way of life here on earth, and our continued integration into God after death. At one level it very much corresponds to the renewal of the covenant in the Book of Exodus when Moses addressed the people of Israel. 'And taking the Book of the Covenant he read it to the listening people ...' (Ex 24:7). Another parallel is found in the Book of Nehemiah, where

> from early morning till noon; all the people listened attentively to the Book of the Law ... And Ezra read from the Law of God, translating and giving the sense, so that the people understood what was read (Neh 8:3, 9).

In our case, when the 'lesson' from scripture is finished, a positive public response is required. When, at the end of the lesson the reader declares: 'The word of the Lord': we respond: 'Thanks be to God.' Before the reading of the Gospel, there is another procession, led by acolytes, with the deacon holding aloft the Book of the Gospels. After the introduction, it is incensed – highlighting its special status. At the end of the gospel reading, the priest kisses the Book of the Gospels and then, holding it aloft, declares: 'The Gospel of the Lord.' However, this part of the Eucharist is more than a didactic element. In the new edition of the Eucharistic Prayer for the Church on the Path of Unity we read:

> Blessed indeed is your Son, present in our midst when we are gathered by his love, and when, as once for the disciples, so now for us, he opens the Scriptures and breaks the bread.

In other words, Christ is present not only in the 'breaking of bread', but in the 'opening of the scriptures'. Indeed, one could speculate, whether or not, at some future date the Church might focus our attention on the presence of Christ during the reading of the sacred scriptures in the Eucharist, by declaring it to be one of the sacraments!

The Preparation of the Gifts
What follows the homily and the Prayer of the Faithful used to be known as the Offertory, but has been downgraded on

the liturgical scale, and is now referred to as the 'Preparation of the Gifts'. Moloney (2003, p. 39), is very clear:

> There is then no room for a little Jewish offering of bread and wine prior to the one great sacrifice of Christ brought before us in the Eucharistic Prayer. The moment of offering and the prayer of offering have to wait, as we will see, for the canon of the Mass.

What comes to mind for most liturgists at this point is the Seder Meal that formed the major part of the Passover Celebration that provided the structure for the Last Supper in the Synoptic Gospels. Apart from establishing this connection, this aspect of the Eucharist lacks any deeper meaning. And Swane (1974, p. 47) concurs:

> A couple of decades ago it was commonplace to hear preachers speak of the offertory as the moment of 'self-offering' when we should place ourselves, spiritually, on the paten and in the chalice. Theologians of the period debated the significance of the offertory. Was it an offering in the strict, i.e. sacrificial sense? An offering of bread and wine? Distinct from the offering of Christ's body and blood? Or was it a mere symbolic anticipation of Christ's offering? The debate has ended. The replacing of the term offering by preparation of the gifts indicates the Church's concern to offset any anticipation of the real offering of sacrifice which takes place during the Eucharistic prayer. It is the offering of Christ, together with his Church, to the Father.

In view of this clarification, it might be no harm to comment on how out of touch it is for celebrants who still continue to lift up the paten and the chalice as high as possible in a dramatic but tawdry gesture of offering, at this point.

The Eucharistic Prayer
The canon of the Mass is now more properly called the Eucharistic Prayer. Irwin (2005, p. 279) tells us:

That this prayer is regarded as the 'centre and summit' of the Eucharist is no surprise. That the GIRM (General Instruction of the Roman Missal, 2005) asserts that it is a prayer the assembly enters into through the power and action of the Holy Spirit is also no surprise.

He notes that the phrase 'the power of the Holy Spirit' did not appear in the first version of the GIRM (2002), and that its inclusion helps ecumenical dialogue. While one could be critical of the new Eucharistic Prayer with regard to style, syntax, rhythm etc., it still evokes a sense of awe as one follows that lovely symmetrical entry into the mystery of Christ's presence and the manifestation of God's love for us through this New Covenant. The pattern is most obvious in Eucharistic Prayer I, with the axis of course being the epiclesis and the consecration (cf. Emminghaus 1988, p. 172–3). The priest performs the traditional rite of placing his hands over the bread and wine. This is of course reminiscent of the solemn dedication in the Hebrew ritual of sacrifice. 'He is to lay his hand on the victim's head, and it shall be accepted as effectual for his atonement' (Lev 1:4). The invocation of the Holy Spirit follows and faith sees on the altar the real presence of the Risen Christ. At this point it is good to recall Crichton's advice regarding symbols and the liturgy.

> The realities it contains and conveys are embodied in certain gestures and in certain things that are used in a special way. We have, in other words, to understand the world of symbol if we are to understand liturgy (1993, p. 19).

The symbols in this case bring to reality the Sacrificed Lamb, prepared in traditional fashion, with the blood drained from the flesh. Once more we bring to mind the image of Christ the Sacrificial Victim with every drop of blood drained from his body, to the extent that finally, only water drains from his pierced side (Jn 19:34).

The great prayer of praise that is the Eucharistic Prayer ends with the doxology and the Great Amen. In commenting on the doxology, Crichton (1976, p. 95) states: 'The Eucharistic prayer began with giving praise and thanksgiving to God through Jesus Christ … The covenant has been renewed …'. This is our Affirmation of Faith: 'Let it be so.' 'We will observe all that Yahweh has decreed; we will obey' (Ex 24:7). The fractured relationship, described in the Book of Genesis, Chapter 3 has now been restored, and in good liturgies, we can detect a change in mood. The fact that at this point we stand is a good indication that something important is going to happen.

The Communion Rite
If ever there were a doubt about the connection between an invitation to a family meal and the strength of the bond or relationship that led to the invitation, then a study of the Communion rite would help clarify it. And so it is no surprise that the GIRM (2005, p. 84) makes it clear that the communion rite begins with the introduction to the Lord's Prayer. This is more than the perfect prayer taught by Jesus to his apostles. In the context of the Eucharist as Covenant, it is one of the most important elements in the liturgy. The 'Our Father' is said with hands outstretched, beginning with an assertion: 'You are our Father in Heaven'. 'Abba', the term that is used would correspond to the word that Irish children would use to address their father – Dad, Daddy, Pa etc. Some liturgists dispute the fact, but 'Abba' is what the modern Israeli child of today uses in similar circumstances. For a people who would not even pronounce the word 'Yahweh' or even write it in pronounceable form, this was a step too far.

But this made the Jews even more intent on killing him, because not content with breaking the Sabbath, he spoke of God as his own Father, and so made himself God's equal (Jn 5:18).

And for us Christians who were reared to fear God, using the familiar 'Dad' when addressing God seems most irreverent and disrespectful. But this is the ultimate spin-off from the covenant that our brother Jesus made between us and God his Father.

The prayer that immediately follows the 'Our Father' mentions in detail the evils from which we beg to be delivered. Then we have the prayer for peace, following which we are afforded the opportunity of showing that we are at peace with our neighbours by offering them a sign of peace. This aspect of the covenant is vital. 'In this way you will be sons of your Father in heaven ...' (Mt 6:45). 'While the Agnus Dei is sung or said ... the principal celebrant breaks the hosts for Communion ...' (GIRM, 2005 p. 85). Being conscious of the traditional division of the covenant victim, the priest will do so with the solemnity that befits this long-established part of the ritual. Juergens (1934, p. 231), while coming from a different perspective, is still conscious of the importance of this action, and tells us:

> At the end of this prayer the Sacred Host is divided to symbolise the immolation of the Victim, the separation of the Body and Soul of Jesus when He died upon Calvary.

The 'commingling' comes next. 'The significance of the mingling with its accompanying (though revised) text remains obscure. It is a rite that could have been omitted without any impoverishment of the communion act' (Crichton 1993, p. 119). However, this insistence on preserving the ancient traditions is reassuring for those who feel that in time its meaning may become clear, with the practice still alive.

The division of the sacrificial victim has been a feature of covenant celebrations from the time of Abram and no doubt, for hundreds of years before that. In all of the General Instructions of the Roman Missal to date, the celebrant has been directed to focus the congregation's attention on the divided host.

> Taking the host, he raises it slightly over the paten and facing the people, says aloud: This is the Lamb of God who takes away the sins of the world. Happy are those who are called to his supper (*The Roman Missal*, 1974).

However, Irwin (2005, p. 161) sees the

> option of holding both the consecrated bread and chalice (as) a helpful ritual adjustment because it combines both bread and cup in what the people look at when they are invited to communion.

But for those who wish to copper-fasten the connection between the Eucharist and the celebration of the New Covenant, the rubric in the New Missal and the GIRM (2005), are disappointing. The New Missal gives a choice that allows the priest to take the host 'and holding it slightly raised above the paten *or above the chalice*, while facing the people', to say the 'Agnus Dei'. The GIRM (No. 243), referring to a concelebrated Eucharist, no longer requires the celebrant to display the divided host:

> Then the principal celebrant takes a host consecrated in the same Mass, holds it slightly raised above the paten or the chalice, and facing the people, says the Agnus Dei …

Another aspect of concelebration is the expectation among the gathered clergy that they will be given a host to hold while the main celebrant holds up the divided host – or more probably, one section of the divided host. This of course fails to preserve, what is after all, a major covenantal tradition. Even worse, is a custom whereby all of the Eucharistic ministers hold up their hosts as the priest asks the people to 'Behold the Lamb of God …'.

There is a saying that has some truth in it: 'We are what we eat.' In Holy Communion we certainly become absorbed into the Body of Christ. In this regard, we could, in imitation of Swayne (1974, p. 73–74), analyse the reception of Holy Communion under the following headings:

> Communion as intimate union with our Lord.
> Communion as a sharing in the redemptive work of Christ.
> Communion as union with one another.

And in fact, this approach was adopted by those who organised the 50th International Eucharistic Congress in 2012. Their banner declared: 'Eucharist: Communion with Christ and with one another.' However, from a covenantal point of view, it might have been better to focus, as Jesus our priest did, on God the Father. Lovers of the New Covenant might have been happier with a banner declaring: 'Union with the Father and with one another, in the love of the Spirit, through Christ our Priest.' As we read the encyclical letter of Pope John Paul II, *Ecclesia de Eucharistia* (2003, p. 33), we can see how this might be more correct:

> The sacrament is an expression of this bond of communion both in its invisible dimension, which, in Christ and through the working of the Holy Spirit, unites to the Father and among ourselves ...

In other words, as we are united to Christ at Holy Communion, we should be aware of the Trinitarian dynamic involved. Through our incorporation into Christ we have access to the Father and are infused with their mutual love – God's Holy Spirit.

When discussing Eucharist as Covenant, Holy Communion is the covenant supper. Christ, the Lamb is sacrificed and eaten, as is the covenant victim whenever a covenant is cut. We could theologise, seeing it as the 'heavenly banquet', the wedding supper of the Lamb', 'the bread of life' etc., but let us not be blind to the essential symbol: it is a covenant meal. Like all communal meals, it carries within itself a potential for a depth of meaning that is universally recognised, though possibly in some societies more than others. In France especially, and in parts of Africa, being invited to a family meal is highly significant. Sitting at table with this family is to be told: 'You are now connected to us. We accept you – "adopt you" as part of our family.' This, of course is an essential part of the covenant process. It is God's family that now sits round the table of the Lord.

At this point, the reception of Holy Communion by the people of God, we come to the perennial problem – reception under one or both species? In this regard, we are unfortunately quite remiss. Even back in 1974, we could read, in the Introduction to the Roman Missal:

> The sign of communion is more complete when given under both kinds, since in that form the sign of the Eucharistic meal appears more clearly. The intention of Christ that the new and eternal covenant be ratified in his blood is better expressed, as is the relation of the Eucharistic banquet to the heavenly banquet.

In the covenant at Sinai, we see both parties sharing the blood of the victim:

> Half of the blood Moses took up and put into basins, the other half he cast on the altar ... Then Moses took the blood and cast it towards the people. 'This', he said 'is the blood of the Covenant Yahweh has made with you ...' (Ex 24:6, 8).

Blood is synonymous with life, but in all cultures we equate shared blood, with being related to one another as family. In a more innocent time, before the arrival of HIV and Aids, many of the American fraternities and sororities, during their initiation ceremonies, after making small incisions in their wrists, mixed their blood to show that they were now part of the brotherhood or sisterhood. In the case of the Hittite Covenants, the participants apparently had the blood spattered on them as they walked between the two halves of the animal victim – thus illustrating their newly-established kinship. In our celebration of the New Covenant, we have an even more powerful symbol of relationship, when we drink the blood of Christ, our Paschal Lamb and Victim. We are now truly integrated into the family of God – brothers and sisters of Christ, with God as our Father.

Holy Communion is a community event, but there is also a process that for each person, whether at the family table or at the liturgy of the Eucharist must take place. To speak of digestion is perhaps a little crude, but there is definitely need for a period of silence, prayer and reflection before the final dismissal. At a lecture in Mary Immaculate College recently, Dr Paula Treacy borrowed a phrase from rugby parlance that helps explain how one might react to wonder and mystery: 'Touch, pause, engage'. Partaking fruitfully in this covenant celebration requires all three 'phases'.

'Who should receive Holy Communion?' This might seem to be a trivial question, to which the answer is obviously: 'Those who are Covenant People.' In practice, however, to go down this road, as one in fairness must, is to enter a maze of issues that continues to plague Christians to this day. Since partaking in the Covenant Meal is an essential part of celebration, the most sensible attitude to adopt is probably that which takes the more positive approach. In other words: We have an obligation to receive Holy Communion unless there is a serious reason why we should not. For many elderly parishioners, a bout of arthritis for example, on a Sunday morning may cause them to 'miss Mass'. Often, they feel unable to receive Holy Communion until they have confessed in the Sacrament of Reconciliation. Another cause for concern often arises at a funeral Mass where someone has previously celebrated at another Eucharist that same day. It must seem obvious that neither of the two instances are reason for not taking part in the banquet. Of course, the critical question arises in the case of members of the other Christian Churches. An attempt will be made to deal with this critical issue in Chapter Seven.

The Dismissal
Finally, as one is dismissed, it is with a sense of joy and amazement that we are children of the Father, united to Him and to one another through our brother Jesus, the Christ, and filled with God's Spirit of love. In the past, the Church members, instead of rushing home, congregated outside the main door. There they met, greeted one another, shared their news, and generally mixed together as a community. How appropriate! In most of the Catholic communities in Britain, a cup of tea and biscuits are served at the back of the church. If we, in Ireland, wish to knit our communities together in a period of diminishing numbers, such communal gatherings would do much to help. Hopefully it will happen more often, as we move from a sense of 'getting Mass on Sunday' to gathering as the Christian community in our own parish church.

Unfortunately, over the years, the people of God have developed a multitude of devotions that are now *de rigour* once Mass is over. Indeed, one can sometimes witness the introduction of the Rosary, the Divine Mercy or some other devotional prayers even while the priest is processing from the altar. The only conclusion one can come to is that these good people feel undernourished after what should be the most wonderful spiritual experience anybody could possibly have.

Is the time right to introduce the Prayer of the Church ten minutes before Mass begins? A possible danger is that while such a move might frustrate the devotional practices of the congregation, it might still not satisfy the affective needs of people who are truly devout and hunger for all that is truly spiritual. If perhaps, those who celebrate Eucharist on a daily basis were more aware of the covenantal structure of the Mass and understood the significance of each act in the Sacred Mysteries, then they might not be so disconnected as to need Novenas to St Anthony or some Marian devotion immediately after the Eucharist to satisfy their spiritual hunger.

Chapter Seven

*How a Covenantal Approach Integrates both Meal and
Sacrifice and may Help Promote Christian Unity*

Eucharistic Elements that Correspond to Covenantal Rites
The initial chapters of this book listed the various ways in
which the Eucharist can be categorised. Most religious
writers choose either to opt for 'sacrifice' or 'meal'. In doing
so, many theologians and liturgists admit to a very real
confusion as to the essential nature of the 'Mass'. However,
the Eucharist is both sacrifice *and* meal – both elements
being essential parts of the structure of the ritual by which
the New and eternal Covenant established by Christ was
celebrated by Him and handed on to us. By taking the
words of Christ literally the problem is solved. At the Last
Supper which ritually and symbolically captured the events
of the *Triduum Sacrum*, we have all the elements that are
germane to a covenant celebration.

The *parties* to this covenant are *God* the Father and all of
humanity. It is a unilateral covenant, i.e. God is the one who
initiates it and is faithful to it, even if we are not.

The *terms* of the covenant are reduced to one. 'I give you
a new commandment: love one another; just as I have loved
you, you also must love one another' (Jn 13:34). *The Liturgy
of the Word* is where this is explained and made relevant for
our community and for each of us as individuals.

Christ is the *priest*. In Eucharistic Prayer IV we recall the
fact that in the past it was through the prophets that the
Heavenly Father had offered us covenants.

And you so loved the world ... that in the fullness of time you sent your only Begotten Son to be our Saviour: And by implication to be the priest who would offer us the New and Eternal Covenant – the one who unites us to God.

He is also the *victim* – the *Lamb of God*, the sacrificed one. But He is a willing victim:

The Father loves me, because I lay down my life in order to take it up again. No one takes it from me; I lay it down of my own free will, and as it is in my power to lay it down, so it is in my power to take it up again; and this is the command I have been given by my Father (Jn 10:17, 18).

The *sacrifice* takes place in the *traditional covenant manner*, with the *body and blood presented separately*.

Tradition also demands that the bloodless body of the *victim* should be *divided*. This takes place before Holy Communion, as the priest holds up *the divided Host* and announces: 'Behold the Lamb of God, behold him who takes away the sins of the world. Blessed are those who are called to the supper of the Lamb.

Holy Communion is the Covenant Meal

We often complain about minimalism in connection with our celebration of the sacraments, and especially when we discuss the Eucharist. Apart from the fact that as a general rule we are not offered the chalice, we often hear the complaint: 'Could the Host not be more substantial, and really have the appearance of bread?' However, if we imagine ourselves back in time at a Hittite covenant celebration, with both tribes making up a considerable number, then the amount of meat offered to each participant would have been quite small. In other words, what we are talking about is a symbolic gesture. And just as the early covenants would have relied on other food sources apart from the flesh of the covenant victim, how difficult would it be to provide an after-Mass cup of tea and biscuits. Such gatherings help our Christian community to get to know each other and to grow in unity, because ever before we are united in the family of God, we must be united with one another. Then we are in a position to form a relationship with the Other.

And of course *relationship* is at the very heart of our covenant. The basic aim of any covenant is the *relationship* formed between the parties involved. Consequently one of the most important parts of the Eucharistic liturgy is where all present stand and claim that wonderful relationship with God by saying: *'Our Father'*. Unfortunately, any casual observer at Mass, focusing on the way this most common of all prayers is recited, could only come to the conclusion that the perfunctory way in which it is 'rattled off' means that it has little or no importance in our celebration. How sad!

Some Considerations Regarding Time
'What should our basic attitude be as we actively take part in the Mass?' Firstly, this covenant that was established once and for all in time and space is now celebrated in sacred time – in the eternal now, and in sacred space – the Heavenly Jerusalem – being neither a renewal nor a repetition of the one and only covenant. 'Anamnesis' is a word that helps give some meaning to what takes place at our Eucharist, deriving as it does from the Jewish practice of living through the experience each time the Passover is celebrated. This allows us to be truly present at this timeless event. In this regard, there is a lot we in the Roman Church can learn from our Orthodox brothers and sisters – that sense of wonder and mystery. Yes! We can intellectualise as we ponder what we observe. Yes! We can examine each aspect of our Eucharistic liturgy and see clearly all the

essential parts of the covenant celebrations that have been described in both Old Testament writings and in historical research. Yes! But ultimately, it is an exercise in love and faith and hope – the living proof of 'the love that the Father has lavished on us' (1 Jn 3:1). However, time-related words are meaningless. We do not *renew* our covenant. We do not go back in time and space. We are not once more at Calvary or at the Last Supper but in the eternal now with Christ in the presence of God the Father, through the power of the Holy Spirit, where we are united with the angels and saints and our own dear dead. And the various Eucharistic Prayers acknowledge this by including us in the hymn of praise:

> And so, with the Angels and all the Saints we declare your glory, as with one voice we acclaim: Holy, Holy, Holy Lord God of hosts.

Two categories of people find this concept of timelessness slightly easier to cope with – those who have studied Einstein's Special Theory of Relativity, and members of the Eastern Churches. The physicists understand that time is a variable, and that our most solid matter is mostly empty space, interchangeable with energy, and liable to increase or decrease depending on its velocity. For them it is slightly easier to imagine a Supreme Being outside of space and time. The Greek and Russian Orthodox churches use a screen behind which the most solemn parts of the liturgy are performed during the Eucharistic celebration. In theory, this helps those present to set themselves before God's throne, where Christ presents his human life eternally in sacrifice to his eternal Father.

The Joy of Celebrating Our Covenant
At a practical level, our realisation that the Eucharist makes real and present the love of God for us, should make a

CHAPTER SEVEN

major difference in the way we celebrate our liturgies of the Eucharist. Perhaps we might imitate the African churches in the way they exhibit joy and verve, and give praise to our Heavenly Father, not only with full hearts and voices in our prayers and hymns, but also by the use of our bodies in sacred gestures, and perhaps even through dance and drumming. However, in this latter regard, we must be careful, and heed the advice given to us in *Sacrosanctum Concilium*. While the Church

> respects and fosters the spiritual adornments and gifts of the various races and peoples ... and sometimes admits such things into the liturgy itself ... they must harmonise with its true and authentic spirit (Abott, 1067, p. 151).

The unfortunate aspect of our Eucharistic celebrations is that they seem to lack energy and enthusiasm. Many of us can still remember our reaction on the night of 30 April 1994 when, during the interval of the Eurovision Song Contest, we saw our national dance performed with such élan and elegance. The challenge for the Irish church is how to put our own stamp on our liturgies, so that it will resonate with our own culture.

Unfortunately, in general, those of us who have spent time in Africa, South America, the Philippines etc. find, on our return to Ireland, that the Mass in our local parish is from a purely affective point of view, unfulfilling. We have, for a long time now, decried the way our teenagers have complained about Mass being boring. Perhaps, we should have listened more to them and tried to understand why, as a whole generation, they had abandoned the Mass. If we had attempted to bring more life and joy to our celebrations then perhaps our churches might not be as empty of young people, as they are at the moment.

How a Covenantal Approach Might Help Christian Unity
Twelve years ago Dorr (2001) wrote as follows:

> Disedifying controversy about inter-communion could perhaps be avoided or lessened by a careful re-thinking of the theology of Eucharist, which underpins the rules.

How true! Apart from the spiritual benefits that would hopefully accrue from embracing a covenantal attitude to the Eucharist, there is also, as mentioned above, an ecumenical dividend. Martos (1981, p. 301), echoing Lafont's sentiments (cf. p. 8), speaks about an inter-church tolerance regarding the Eucharist that has developed since the 1960s and the changes in theological thinking that has made this possible. He wrote:

> At the same time scholars in the biblical movement rediscovered the connection between the last supper and the scriptural ideas of covenant, meal, and Passover, and since these connections were found in the Bible, the hierarchy had no objection to them.

Were such an approach to the celebration to help us in the process of reunification, then Christ's best wish would be well on the road to fulfilment:

> that they may be one like us ... May they all be one. Father, may they be one in us ... With me in them and you in me, may they be so completely one that the world may realise that it was you who sent me and that I have loved them as much as you loved me (Jn 17:11, 21–3).

Looking through the Vatican II documents one can detect a certain dynamic toward unity among the Christian churches. *Lumen Gentium* is particularly warm in the way it acknowledges that we are 'joined in many ways to the baptized who are honoured by the name of Christian ...' (15). And while some parts of the Decree on Ecumenism (*Unitatis Redintegratio*) seem overly legalistic and make reference for example to situations where the 'unity of sacramental faith is deficient', there are also some positive statements. We read with regard to the other Christian Churches in the West, that

> when they commemorate the Lord's death and resurrection in the Holy Supper, they profess that it signifies life in communion with Christ and they await his coming in glory. For these reasons, dialogue should be undertaken concerning the true meaning of the Lord's Supper, the other sacraments and the Church's worship and ministry (n. 22).

In this regard, if all the Christian Churches were to focus on the Eucharist as Covenant, it would certainly help. In the covenant approach, there are occasions when we can move away from the local parish and denominational aspects of the celebration and enter into sacred time and space – the eternal now. Here we are members of

> a huge number, impossible to count, of people from every nation, race, tribe and language ... standing in front of the throne and in front of the Lamb ... (Rev 7:9).

Of course, we are members of the parish Christian community, and every weekend we gather as one. We expect to see our neighbours, hear about the things that affect them, get the newsletter that tells us of local happenings that are of relevance to the parish, and of course, celebrate Eucharist in the way that is familiar to us over the years.

We pray for N. our Pope and N. our Bishop, very conscious that they are our religious leaders. But there can be other religious gatherings, marking special events when we are more conscious that God has 'cut' His covenant with us as a people and makes 'no distinction between Jew and Greek ... for everyone who calls on the name of the Lord will be saved' (Rom 10:13). Would it be a grave offence to the Lord if, at the wedding of a Catholic bride and a Church of Ireland groom, all present received the Eucharist? True! In *Unitatis Redintegratio* we read that:

> Of its very nature the celebration of the Eucharist signifies the fullness of profession of faith and the fullness of ecclesial communion (Flannery, ed., 1975, p. 557)

We also read that 'ecclesial communion' is a vital aspect of our fellowship within the Christian community. But there are times when we all have to ask ourselves the question: 'What would Jesus do?' When the Lord broke bread, it was not always with those who had the approval of 'the competent religious authority', but these meals were by definition, a sacramental celebration. As members of a church where we have grown up in a comfortable certainty where clear rules have governed every aspect of Catholic belief and practice, perhaps we should sometimes, as mentioned above, ask ourselves what the mind of Christ might be and act accordingly. Personally, I feel that if we move to a covenantal approach in celebrating Eucharist, these rigid boundaries will become less of an obstacle to intercommunion.

Please God, this dialogue will continue. Considering the scandal that divided Christianity gives to all – people of good will, as well as those opposed to the Gospel – if a covenant approach to the Eucharist were to help us along the road to unity, what a miracle would be achieved! Finally, if this book has convinced even a few worshippers of the value of adopting a covenantal approach when celebrating *Our Splendid Eucharist*, then the energy and time spent on this work will have been well worth it.